The Rickenbacker Electric Bass

50 Years as Rock's Bottom

Paul D. Boyer

Hal Leonard Books

An Imprint of Hal Leonard Corporation

Published in 2013 by Hal Leonard Books
An Imprint of Hal Leonard Corporation
7777 West Bluemound Road
Milwaukee, WI 53213

Trade Book Division Editorial Offices
33 Plymouth St., Montclair, NJ 07042

All photos by Paul D. Boyer unless otherwise credited

Printed in China through Colorcraft Ltd., Hong Kong

Book design by Paul D. Boyer
Cover and foldout design by Tonya J. Limberg

Library of Congress Cataloging-in-Publication Data

Boyer, Paul D. (Paul Donald), 1949-
 The Rickenbacker electric bass : 50 years as rock's bottom / Paul D. Boyer.
    pages cm
1. Rickenbacker guitar--History. 2. Bass guitar--History. I. Title.
 ML1015.G9B69 2013
 787.87'19--dc23
                       2013001013

ISBN 978-1-4768-8680-0

www.halleonardbooks.com

Contents

About this book

I first became aware of Rickenbacker basses when I pored over the pictures of the Beatles in the "Magical Mystery Tour" LP jacket in 1967. There, Paul McCartney is fingering a bass that was not his usual Höfner! What is that? I wondered. Little did I know that I had been listening to McCartney's Rickenbacker 4001S bass since the *Rubber Soul* album was released in 1965. While I had noticed sonic improvement in the bass lines, I imagined it was improved recording technology rather than a change of instrument.

If I had been more observant, I would have seen Rickenbacker's counter-invasion of basses in the hands of other British players: the Kinks' Peter Quaife, the Who's John Entwistle, Pink Floyd's Roger Waters, and others.

My second occasion to notice a Rickenbacker bass was in 1972, in the photos of the booklet included in "Fragile," the breakout album by Britain's progressive-rock band Yes. The band's bassist, Chris Squire, generated massive, grinding overtones from the instrument, quite different from McCartney's full, clean, plunking sound. Same instrument – completely different sound.

If you were a bassist in a rock band in the 1970s, you just had to have a "Rick." And since I was a bassist in a band in the '70s, I had to have one, too. I bought a used 1972 Mapleglo 4001 in 1975, and have held onto it ever since. It sat under the guest bed for decades until my interest was rekindled in 2002.

With the rise of the Internet in the new millennium, I became aware of chat groups for Rickenbacker enthusiasts and collectors. Chief among them was the Rickenbacker Resource Forum (www.rickresource.com/forum). The participants there provided a wealth of knowledge and experience, but also a lot of conflicting information.

There was no dedicated reference on Rickenbacker basses, just bits and pieces in books on guitars and in Richard R. Smith's *The Complete History of Rickenbacker Guitars* (1987). What was needed was an up-to-date, comprehensive field guide to Rickenbacker basses – a book that would clearly illustrate all the different bass models and their features. Some historical background was needed as well.

With my 24 of years experience as writer and editor at Kalmbach Publishing Co. and my background in photog-raphy, I saw the creation of a reference on Rickenbacker basses as the ideal retirement project.

The Rickenbacker Electric Bass – 50 Years As Rock's Bottom is the result of nine years of accumulating photos and digesting information from myriad sources. I could spend many more years gathering, but eventually the preparation work for a book has to pause and the publishing has to occur so the information can get to the reader.

This book is as accurate as I could make it, but it's likely that additional information will surface to contradict or supplement what is here. Corrections and additions are welcome and may be submitted to the author or publisher for possible use in a revised edition.

No absolutes

Rickenbacker International Corp. (RIC) is a privately held company, and as such, business details such as production numbers and financials were not available to this author. With the exception of declared limited-production models, there is no way to establish how many of a certain instrument were made at any time. Earlier publications have included production numbers based on early company sales receipts, but it has never been shown that those records are complete. My assessments of instruments' rarity are based on field and market encounters, or on official correspondence from company management.

Timelines

The instruments' production timelines stated throughout the book are based on company catalogs, price sheets, and dating examples in the field. There's a lot of gray area here, because the company would gradually phase out the availability of models, features, or colors as inventory or orders dictated. Once in a while, an instrument will exhibit a feature or color that seems out of its timeline. This may occur with the fulfillment of an order for a special customer (individual or dealer), or the whim of management with a supply of spare parts and paint tins. It is best to consider Rickenbacker model, feature, and color timelines as "soft" – no hard and fast beginning or end dates.

(Below) 2010 4003 in Midnight Blue. Portrait by Bill Henshell.

Fretless basses

RIC considers fretless Rickenbacker basses as separate models in sales brochures/catalogs and price sheets (4001FL and later the 4003FL). However, I treat fretless as an optional feature in this book. Scattered throughout these pages are photos of fretless 3001, 4000, 4001S, 4002, and 4003S basses which were never mentioned as separate models in company literature. Fretless basses differ only in the fingerboard, so I have illustrated them within the chapters of their "parent" model, rather than as separate models.

Acknowledgments

The writing of a book is credited to the author, and the production to the publisher, but it is impossible for them to create a reference book such as this from thin air. Contributors of data and photos from around the world made this book happen, and my sincere gratitude goes to all. Without the cooperation of John Hall, Cindalee Hall, Ben Hall, Geoff Chapluk, Kenny Howes, Richard Cannata, Dan Beighley, and the crew at Rickenbacker International Corp., the book would be incomplete. As owners and employees of the company, it is not in their job descriptions to help with an effort outside of their business. So their contributions are especially appreciated.

Without the help of the publishers, this book would still be just a dream in a computer. Thanks to Brad Smith, Mike Edison, John Cerullo, Carol Flannery, and Clare Cerullo at Hal Leonard Books for making it a reality. And thanks to Tonya Limberg for the cover designs and invaluable help with software training and advice on page layout design. A special shout out goes to John Biscuti, John Hall, and Jeff Scott for their sharp eyes during fact check, and to Mark Hembree for his excellent copy edit.

Collectors and experts were also instrumental (pun intended) in ensuring the usefulness of this book. Principally, participants of the Rick Resource Forum lent their considerable knowledge to this author. My thanks go especially to Katie Adams, John Alekna, John Allgaier, Brenda Almond, Mark Arnquist, Scott Baillie, Chris Becker, Richard Bengston, Howard Bishop, Jim Blake, Larry Bolt, Jim Boyle, Tim Bugbee, Dick Burke, Al Cisneros, Gary Clauson, Chris Clayton of Pick of the Ricks, Eileen Colton, Steve Cooper, Brian Crisman, Tony D'Amico, Joseph Deas of Olivia's Vintage, Susan Daley, Chris Dekker, Marlon Deppen, Frank Paul DiCamillo, Scott Doseck, Tony Dudzik of Pickguardian, Ken Earnest, Steven Fant, Tony Felgueiras Photography, Fran Festa, Dave Fisher, Dale Bruce Fortune, Jim Glen, Charley Goehring, Graham Griffiths, Mike Gutierrez, Gary Hahlbeck of North Coast Music, Lindsay Hahn, Chris Harris, Hasbro, Inc., Randy Hawkins, Joe Hayes, Bert Heitling, Don Henderson, Bill Henshell, Heritage Auction Galleries, Ed Hoffer, Gareth Holder, Sheree Homer, Amy Humphrey, Terry Hungerford, International Vintage Guitars, Steve Jennings, CJ Johansson, Ken Joseph, Jerry Juden, Oyama Katsuyuki, Robin Kauffman, Eduardo Kelerstein, Graham King, James Kirkland, John H. Koelling, Erik Kutzler, Kevin Lang, Peter Levett, Andy Lewis, Rudy Lu, Dan Machnik, Eden MacKenzie, Dan MacPherson, Ian D. Martin, Tony Matura, Joe Mazurek, Peter McCormack of Rick Resource, David McDonald, Jason Mendelson, Mark Mendoza, Dean Mentjes, Ron Meyer, Paul Michaels, Jaymi Millard, John Minutaglio, Jonathan Mole, Simon Mole, Mandy L. Montanye/Music Go Round, Brian Morton, Donald Mouck, Paul Mutchler, Jared Nakanishi, Teresa Nemr, Irwan Notosoetarso of Fotono Photography, Ron O'Keefe, Chris Pappas, Mike Parks of The Rickenbacker Page/Music Connection, Dave Pascoe, John Peterson, Ken Pierogg, Steve Pitkin/Pitkin Studio, Chris Poteat, Daniele Purrone, Jeff Rath, John Rickinger, Ronn Roberts, Rock Star Guitars, GingerDawn Seaboyer, Marc Seligman, Kenneth Siegel, John Simmons, Chris Squire, Ted Staberow, Eddie Stubbs, Jim Summaria Photography, Ken Swearingen, Dennis Taylor, Kevin Teed, Jeff Thomas, Mark Thompson, Darren Trott, Karin van de Wiel, Joey Vasco, Wade's Guitar Shop, Krista Wallhagen, Stacey Warnke, Dave Westheimer, Paul Wilczynski, Dane Wilder, Wildwood Guitars, John Williams, Andrew Winter, Josh Withers, Steve Wood, Paul Yan, and Bob Young.

Dedication

For Dorothy

For providing a space for this project in your life,
allowing a room for the Ricks in our home,
and granting a place for me in your heart.

Introduction

Rickenbacker's iconic bass guitar was not the first to hit the market – most people credit Fender and its equally iconic Precision model as the pioneer in the market. However, it was the inventors within the precursors of the Rickenbacker International Corp. who helped make the electric bass a possibility. They developed the first practical electric pickup in the 1930s, allowing the "electric guitar" to bring music out of the parlor and into the amphitheatre. The electric pickup allowed the guitar (and eventually the bass) to evolve from a vague undertone in the rhythm section to a lead instrument and driving force behind modern music.

New sound

Although many experimented with modified microphones and phonograph-needle assemblies in the 1920s, it was George Beauchamp who in 1931 developed the practical magnetic electrical coil pickup that became the model to those that followed. Beauchamp was a musician who worked with John Dopyera (who with his brothers lent his name to the resophonic guitar Dobro) to found the National String Instrument Corporation in 1928 in Los Angeles, California. Together, they designed and produced metal resonators that mechanically amplified the sound of otherwise traditional guitars.

George Beauchamp.

The production of many of the metal parts used in these resonators was contracted to the Rickenbacher Manufacturing Co. That shop's owner, Adolph "Rick" Rickenbacher, was also an investor with National.

After several corporate shifts, Beauchamp and Rickenbacher in 1931 founded a new company called Ro-Pat-In Corporation to produce instruments using his new pickups. Beauchamp's 1934 patent (let in 1937) shows the original "Frying Pan" design of the world's first production electric guitar. He set up a new shop in Los Angeles, right next door to Rickenbacher. The early electric guitars from Ro-Pat-In were known as "Electro String" instruments. By 1934, the company name was changed to the Electro-String Instrument Corporation. The company produced electrified "Hawaiian" guitars (played on the lap with a steel slide) and "Spanish" guitars (traditional) in the 1930s and '40s. Rickenbacher invested in Electro-String, and shared in the manufacturing process. The label on these early instruments read "Rickenbacher Electro."

By the late 1930s, began tó substitute the "h" in Rickenbacher with a "k" to avoid association with the great unpleasantness then descending on Europe.

Beauchamp also experimented with electrifying other musical instruments, and developed radically new electric violins, violas, cellos, and bass viols, all using variations of his revolutionary "horseshoe" pickup. Not many of these early bass viols were made, and few exist today, but the concept of the electrically amplified bass was born.

Eventually, Beauchamp tired of the business and sold off his interest in 1940. Electro-String carried on producing instruments, first from cast aluminum and later from Bakelite and stamped metal. The factory produced armatures for gyroscopes during World War II, returning to instrument production in 1946. But interest in electric Hawaiian guitars waned postwar, and by the early 1950s Adolf Rickenbacker was ready to sell the business and retire.

An electric bass viol with a Rickenbacker Horseshoe pickup. Jeff Scott photo. All other photos, RIC archives.

New direction

The buyer was Francis C. Hall, who took over just in time to take advantage of new markets for

Francis C. Hall (left) and Adolf Rickenbacker reminiscing with the "Frying Pan" – the original electric guitar.

electrified music in jazz, rhythm & blues, and the new "rock and roll." Hall's established company, the Radio & Television Equipment Co., was coincidently the distributor for instruments produced by fellow Californian Leo Fender. Hall ended that relationship about a year after he took over Electro-String in December 1953.

F.C. Hall revamped the company and its line of instruments, and with the help of Paul Barth and Roger Rossmeisl, he developed the new instruments that formed the core of the Rickenbacker line that carries on today. Hall, Barth, and Rossmeisl were responsible for the design and development of the Rickenbacker basses, starting in the mid-1950s.

Roger Rossmeisl.

Hall consolidated the factory, warehouse, and headquarters to a new facility in Santa Ana, California, in 1964. With the growing popularity of Rickenbacker instruments then being played by the Beatles, the Byrds, and other pop music groups, Hall changed the name of the company to the more apropos Rickenbacker, Inc.

Rickenbacker today

F.C. Hall retired in 1984 and sold the business to his son John, and his wife, Cindalee, who are now the sole owners. The transition also brought about the current company name, Rickenbacker International Corp. (RIC).

With the exception of some German-made tuners and bridges and a few electronic components, Rickenbacker basses are manufactured and assembled in the USA. Unlike Fender and Gibson, the Halls have neither sought nor needed to shift production of any of their instruments to foreign countries.

Rickenbacker International Corporation.

Today, RIC is housed in a single building on Main Street in downtown Santa Ana. Surrounded by office buildings and freeways, the Halls, along with their son Ben and dozens of talented and dedicated craftsmen and women, continue to produce Rickenbacker instruments.

Rickenbacker basses

F.C. Hall, Paul Barth, and Roger Rossmeisl started toying with a fretted electric bass design as early as 1953. Fender had introduced its successful Precision bass in 1951, and clearly there was room in the market for a competing instrument. Early Rickenbacker basses were handmade with components of six-string guitars. Archival brochures and price sheets suggest that the initial bass model, the 4000, wasn't marketed until 1957. Surviving examples from the 1950s are exceedingly rare. There probably wasn't a "first" example of the 4000, but more likely several experimentals that were repeatedly modified, dismantled, and reassembled to test design ideas and functions.

Ruby 4003 basses await final assembly.

With the introduction of the two-pickup 4001 model in 1961, sales of Rickenbacker basses started to pick up. Large pop bands became smaller "groups," and more groups depended on electric basses to support the bottom end of their sound. The Beatles' use of Rickenbacker instruments was pivotal: Teen groups everywhere wanted to have the same instruments the Beatles used so they could achieve the "right" sound.

Progressive rock groups that flourished in the late 1960s and '70s discovered new sounds that could be generated with the Rickenbacker bass, and sales continued to grow. All along, RIC tweaked the design and hardware of its flagship 4001, and introduced other models to satisfy the ever-widening market. Lower-priced models, hollow-body basses, double-neck guitar/bass instruments, and more streamlined designs brought the selection of Rickenbacker basses to as many as a dozen different models in the late '80s and early '90s.

For years, RIC has accomplished its own distribution, selling directly to a firm network of established retail dealers around the globe. Today, Rickenbacker enjoys an interesting "problem": Demand for its instruments exceeds production capacity, even with advanced computer-aided design and machining tools. As a result, RIC has streamlined production, paring down bass selection to the flagship 4003 (which took over top position from the 4001 after 1980), and the more modern 4004 models.

The future for the Rickenbacker bass might look a lot like its past. Production of the standard deluxe 4003 with its ever-retro look may be accompanied by a return of a "vintage" model soon.

The 4000 Bass

1957 – 1984

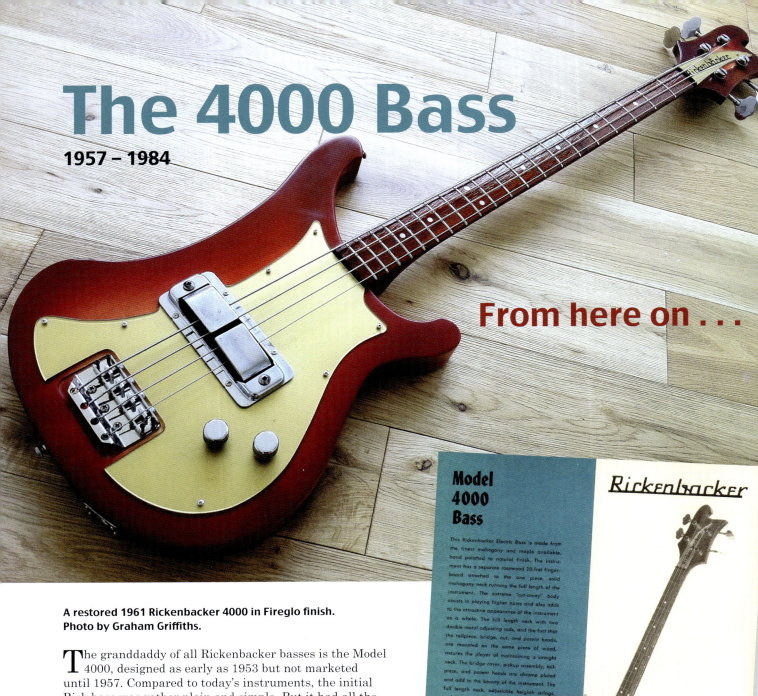

From here on . . .

**A restored 1961 Rickenbacker 4000 in Fireglo finish.
Photo by Graham Griffiths.**

The granddaddy of all Rickenbacker basses is the Model 4000, designed as early as 1953 but not marketed until 1957. Compared to today's instruments, the initial Rick bass was rather plain and simple. But it had all the hallmarks of its progeny, including the "cresting wave" shape of the upper and lower body wings, repeated in miniature on the four-peg headstock. Construction comprised a mahogany plank that started at the headstock and ran all the way to the butt end of the body. This "neck-through-body" design meant that both ends of the bass strings were anchored to a single wooden assembly. The design had advantages – distinctive tone and increased sustain.

The "wings" of the body and headstock were milled to shape and glued to the full-length neck. The fingerboard was rosewood with pearlescent dot position markers.

Early examples of the 4000 used off-the-shelf parts, including a rather simple tailpiece, still exhibiting six anchor points as used on electric six-string guitars.

A novel adjustable string mute was provided. The gadget slid fore and aft on the strings inside acrylic brackets. In the aft position, the foam-rubber mute rested behind the

The Rickenbacker catalog from 1957 announces the new model 4000 bass. RIC archives.

bridge. Slid forward in the brackets, the mute sat on top of the strings ahead of the bridge.

The 4000 featured Rickenbacker's patented "Horseshoe" magnetic pickup, controlled by single rotating volume and tone knobs.

The 1957 Rickenbacker catalog read: "This Rickenbacker Electric Bass is made from the finest mahogany and maple available, hand polished to natural finish. The instrument has a separate rosewood 20-fret fingerboard attached to the one piece, solid mahogany neck running the full length of the instrument. The extreme 'cut-away' body assists in playing higher notes and also adds to the attractive appearance of the instrument as a whole. The full length neck with two double metal adjusting rods, and the fact that the tailpiece, bridge, nut, and patent heads, are mounted on the same piece of wood, assures the player of maintaining a straight neck. The bridge cover, pickup assembly, tailpiece, and patent heads are chrome plated and add to the beauty of the instrument. The full length neck, adjustable height strings, and individual adjustments for string length assures the player of perfect pitch and intonation for each string. This instrument has the famous Rickenbacker pickup unit combined with separate volume and tone controls. The physical size of the electric bass makes

(Above) A trade-show model in crinoline displays what was probably one of the first Rickenbacker 4000 basses. Likely only the first few prototypes had the output jack on the face of the instument next to the volume and tone knobs. (Left) 4000 basses were first available in a "natural" finish, but Rickenbacker applied its signature color, Fireglo, to the 4000 starting about 1960. This example basks in the setting sun outside the company headquarters. RIC photos.

it more portable than the conventional acoustical bass, and still it produces more volume."

The creators

In a 2008 interview, Rickenbacker International Corp. CEO John Hall provided some background on the genesis of the Model 4000:

"The 4000 was (created at) the specific request of F.C. Hall, who had been told by the sales staff and musicians that there was a need for such an instrument. This was tasked to Roger Rossmiesl through Paul Barth, the factory manager at Electro-String, and not an inconsiderable designer in his own right. Rossmiesl developed the general lines of the body of the instrument, while Barth worked on the hardware. F.C. Hall worked on the circuitry and

(Above) Las Vegas and television stars in the early 1960s, the Fabulous Kim Sisters pose with an all Rickenbacker lineup, including the 4000 bass. RIC photo.

(Left) The backside of this 1959 4000 contrasts the walnut neck-through-body assembly with the maple body wings. Early 4000s were finished in "natural" or with a brown burst. Graham Griffiths photo.

pickup configuration. In the end, I would say that Roger Rossmiesl gave birth to the unique character that the series has, Paul Barth gave it the utility, and F.C. Hall the sound.

"Work began on this project in 1953, and various prototypes began to appear in April of 1954. There rarely is one prototype; perhaps there's the first one to go through to completion, but there's always a handful of test bodies, parts samples, and test beds for pickups and stringing in the process. Some of these hung in the rafters at the Western Ave. factory (in Los Angeles), but I presume they were disposed of when the factory moved to Santa Ana. I am not aware of 'the prototype' existing as such."

As design of the bass progressed, the wood used for the neck-through construction was changed. Hall again:

"Mahogany was a traditional wood that Rossmiesl liked to use, but it requires special preparation of the wood in the finishing process that the factory did not

10

(Above) This early 1960s photo shows Jimmy Luttrell and the Vagabond Trio with a rare Model 4000 in Fireglo that had binding and shark-fin position markers normally found on the twin-pickup 4001. RIC photo.

(Right) Another rare bird: This 1962 Model 4000 features the new, thinner body and extended upper horn while retaining the original pick guard and bridge/mute assembly. Note the surround for the pickup is the flared type as found on Rickenbacker steel guitars. Photo by Teresa Nemr & Mark Mendoza.

want to do. It was also somewhat heavy, and it was thought walnut might be lighter and easier to finish. At the same time, maple was being used for guitar bodies, so the transition to a common wood that satisfied all of these criteria was inevitable."

Sales of the new Rickenbacker bass began in the late 1950s. Hall reckons:

"The 4000 first appears on a regular pricelist in July, 1958. However, the December 1957 sales kits also feature the Model 4000 prominently. Given the fact that trade shows in that era were generally held during the summer, and that price lists often lagged one marketing cycle behind, I'll suggest that it was introduced officially at the 1956 summer NAMM (National Association of Music Merchants) show. Photos from some smaller shows also show basses being displayed in 1955. I also have seen some documents dated 1954 which suggests work on the bass was well underway, and that's entirely consistent with my father's plan, beginning in late 1953, to fully revamp the product line."

Design changes

As production ramped up in the early 1960s, the Rickenbacker designers incorporated a few improvements.

Pioneer Player

Among early 4000 players was James Kirkland, bassist for Rick Nelson in the late 1950s and with country star Jim Reeves in the early 1960s. Kirkland's two-tone brown 4000 was given to him in 1958 by F.C. Hall when Rickenbacker was sponsoring Rick Nelson.

In a 2012 phone interview, Kirkland stated "I received the bass along with an amplifier for it. It was the best bass I ever played. The Horseshoe pickup had great tone. The only thing I didn't like was that it was neck heavy."

Kirkland played the Rickenbacker on recordings and in live performances. By 1960, he had left Nelson and joined "Gentleman Jim" Reeves and the Blue Boys. His bass was refinished in Nashville to a powder-blue color that matched the other Rickenbacker guitars then used by the Blue Boys. Kirkland recalls, "I was one of the first to play electric bass on stage at the Grand Ole Opry. That was June of 1960."

According to the Rockabilly Hall of Fame profile, James Kirkland became disenchanted with the Nashville scene and left his Rick bass and amplifier in Reeves' basement. Reeves was killed in a plane crash in 1964. Kirkland said, "I was fed up with the music business and left it for good. I didn't care about that bass when I left Nashville, but I'd sure like have it back now!" The location of Kirkland's famous Rickenbacker remains a mystery.

(Top) James Kirkland plays an early Rickenbacker 4000 while backing up Rick Nelson in 1959 along with James Burton on Rickenbacker pedal steel guitar. Kirkland later went to Nashville to back up "Gentleman Jim" Reeves (left center) and the Blue Boys. The all-Rickenbacker lineup was finished in light blue – even the grille cloth on the amplifiers! RIC photos.

4000 (early production) Identifying Features

Closeup views of a 1962 4000 show that the truss rod cover was carved out to fit around the E and D tuning posts. Note the unslotted tuning pegs. Below, a tail-end shot shows details of the sliding mute cover and original Horseshoe pickup. Detail photos by Teresa Nemr & Mark Mendoza. Main photo by Graham Griffiths.

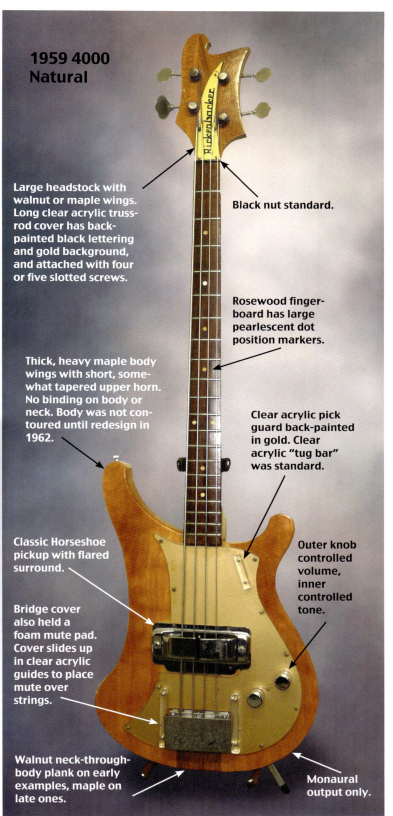

1959 4000 Natural

Large headstock with walnut or maple wings. Long clear acrylic truss-rod cover has back-painted black lettering and gold background, and attached with four or five slotted screws.

Black nut standard.

Rosewood finger-board has large pearlescent dot position markers.

Thick, heavy maple body wings with short, some-what tapered upper horn. No binding on body or neck. Body was not con-toured until redesign in 1962.

Clear acrylic pick guard back-painted in gold. Clear acrylic "tug bar" was standard.

Classic Horseshoe pickup with flared surround.

Outer knob controlled volume, inner controlled tone.

Bridge cover also held a foam mute pad. Cover slides up in clear acrylic guides to place mute over strings.

Walnut neck-through-body plank on early examples, maple on late ones.

Monaural output only.

13

They first reduced the weight of the instrument by trimming the thickness of the body from approximately 1⁵⁄₈" (41mm) to about 1¼" (31mm). This affected the balance, so the upper "horn" of the body was extended a bit to keep the instrument from being neck heavy. The chrome-plated surround for the pickup varied over the years; some were a simple rounded-corner rectangle, some had a flared extension toward the bridge.

The new bridge/tailpiece assembly, with an under-string mute, and the new-style pick guard of the deluxe two-pickup 4001 were eventually applied to the single-pickup 4000 bass, probably late in 1962 or early 1963.

An early 1960s photo of the Vagabond Trio shows a Fireglo 4000 bass with original hardware but featuring the deluxe pearlescent "shark fin" position markers and white-bound body and neck. These deluxe trim items became standard on the two-pickup 4001.

After 1968, the vaunted "Horseshoe" pickup was replaced by the company's new "High-gain" unit with its "faux-horseshoe" cover.

Set-neck Rick

It was not until mid-1972 that Rickenbacker modified the design once again. This time, the famous "neck-through" construction was replaced by a set-neck design. This allowed the bodies to be made from a two-piece slab of maple instead of a pair of body wings glued to the neck-through assembly. It was also a feature of the 4001S model in that timeframe, so either model could be made from this common chassis. All bass necks were made with a center strip of shedua at this time, and it is visible in see-through finishes such as Mapleglo, Fireglo, and Burgundy – just in the neck, not in the body.

Demand for the single-pickup 4000 dwindled through the 1970s as the twin-pickup 4001 became more popular, and production eventually ceased in the early 1980s.

This pair of 4000 basses exhibit design changes in the late 1960s and '70s. The 1968 Mapleglo on the left shows the new tailpiece / bridge / mute design that debuted in 1962. The headstock still carries the walnut "head wings." Note yet another shape for the pickup surround. Also, the pick guard extends all the way down to the surround. On the right is a very rare fretless set-neck 4000, a 1977 model in Burgundy. The shedua strip is visible on the stockier headstock of the 1970s. The pickup is the more modern High-gain unit with its "faux Horseshoe" cover. Note the pick guard doesn't reach the pickup surround.

4000 (and 4001S) basses from mid-1972 to the end of production in the early '80s had a set-neck construction. The neck was shaped to fit into a pocket cut in the body. The joint at the face of the body is seen here with the pick guard removed. Note the shedua strip in the center of the neck. The circular impression is likely from a C-clamp that held the joint together while the glue set.

The set-neck joint is not flush with the back of the body. The central shedua strip makes a strong "three-piece" neck. Ron O'Keefe photos.

4000 (late production) Identifying Features

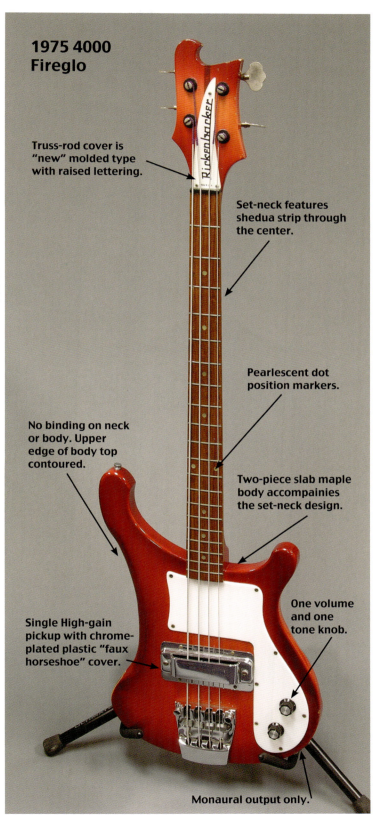

1975 4000 Fireglo

Truss-rod cover is "new" molded type with raised lettering.

Set-neck features shedua strip through the center.

Pearlescent dot position markers.

No binding on neck or body. Upper edge of body top contoured.

Two-piece slab maple body accompainies the set-neck design.

Single High-gain pickup with chrome-plated plastic "faux horseshoe" cover.

One volume and one tone knob.

Monaural output only.

4001
"THE"
Rickenbacker bass
1961 – 1984

To many guitar aficionados, collectors, and players, the 4001 is the only bass from Rickenbacker. Those not so "in the know" mistake current models for the classic 4001. Indeed, the deluxe, twin-pickup 4001 was the flagship of Rick's bass lineup (if not the entire fleet of instruments) for more than 20 years.

It is a reasonable assumption that the development of the 4001 was in response to the 1960 debut of the twin-pickup Jazz Bass from Fender. But it was also a logical progression from the plain, single-pickup 4000. Designers at Rickenbacker retained the shapes of the original and dressed it up with deluxe features found on the company's top-end guitars.

(Above) Company president F.C. Hall (right) and salesmen display the new 4001 bass at a trade show in 1963. RIC photo. (Left) A beautifully preserved example of the deluxe Fireglo 4001 bass from 1968.

A   B   C   D   E

Development

You can see the progression of the design from the original 4000 (A) to the standard 4001 (E) among a few rare examples and photos. The first step was the reduction of weight and extension of the upper "horn" (B). The next step seems to be shown in a snapshot of the Vagabond Trio (page 11) playing a single-pickup bass with appointments usually found on Rickenbacker's top-of-the-line guitars; checker ("block") binding and triangular ("shark fin") position markers on the fingerboard (C in artist's concept).

The installation of a second Horseshoe pickup would have been immediately discounted, as it would severely restrict players' access to the strings, add weight, and look rather unattractive! But Rickenbacker's alternate Toaster-top pickup (also called "Chrome Bar" in company literature) was chosen, set in a newly routed recess and attached to the pick guard. This was a guitar pickup with six magnetic slugs mounted underneath, but the only changes needed were to cut the magnets a bit shorter and revamp the baseplate so it could hold mounting screws to the pick guard (D).

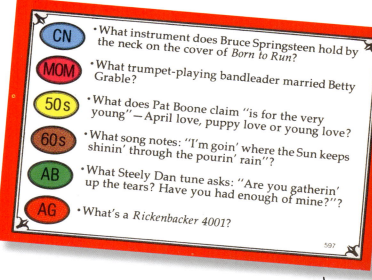

CN • What instrument does Bruce Springsteen hold by the neck on the cover of *Born to Run*?

MOM • What trumpet-playing bandleader married Betty Grable?

50s • What does Pat Boone claim "is for the very young"—April love, puppy love or young love?

60s • What song notes: "I'm goin' where the Sun keeps shinin' through the pourin' rain"?

AB • What Steely Dan tune asks: "Are you gatherin' up the tears? Have you had enough of mine"?

AG • What's a *Rickenbacker 4001*?

597

While playing Trivial Pursuit with friends in 1985, the author was asked the bottom question on this card from the RPM edition. He answered with a show-and-tell of his own 4001.
TRIVIAL PURSUIT® & ©2011 Hasbro, Inc. Used with permission.

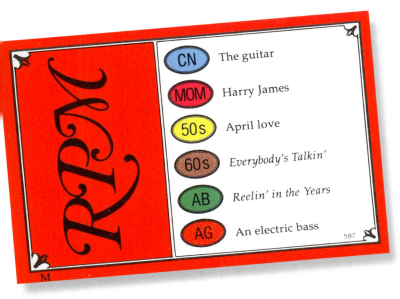

Bet you knew the answer, too!
TRIVIAL PURSUIT ® & ©2011 Hasbro, Inc.
Used with permission.

One of the earliest twin-pickup Rickenbackers is this gorgeous November 1961 example (above) that surfaced for a February 2011 auction. It spans a gap in the design development of the quintessential 4001 bass. It has the deluxe appointments, thinner body with the long upper horn, and two pickups, but retains the early bridge/mute assembly, pick guard, and curiously, only a single set of volume and tone controls. There was no pickup selector toggle-switch fitted either, so both pickups were always activated.

New bridge

It's not clear when Rickenbacker brought its characteristic bridge/tailpiece to the design, but likely it was early in 1962. The new unit was first cast in aluminum and provided an under-string mute that allowed the player to raise or lower the foam pad by turning two thumbscrews. A recess next to the mute held a newly designed bridge. Separate cast saddles could move fore and aft in slots cut into the top of the bridge, with intonation adjusted by screws at the rear of the bridge.

The new unit required shallow routings in the body to make way for the mute and bridge, so a redesign of the plastic pick guard was done. The utility of separate volume and tone controls for each pickup and a three-way toggle was clear, so the control cavity was enlarged. The route for the wires to the new "neck" pickup was accomplished with multiple bores of a Forstner bit in a drill press.

18

This twin-pickup Rickenbacker bass is clearly a developmental example rather than a full-scale production unit. Issued in November of 1961, it exhibits a late stage in the progressive changes on the way to the classic 4001. Photo by Heritage Auction Galleries.

On your mark

Through the years, the factory slowly refined the 4001. Most of the changes were cosmetic, such as the material used for the "shark fin" position markers on the finger-board. The early examples were a pearlescent material, likely cut from sheet stock and glued into depressions cut in the board. Some of these markers appear quite plain, almost a solid white.

Starting about 1964 and continuing until early 1973, the company produced markers known as "crushed pearl." These sparkly markers were popular among play-ers and collectors, but the sheet material was difficult to cut and install. Also, the full-width routes for them in the fingerboard were compromising the stiffness of the neck, making for problems when the increasingly popular round-wound RotoSound strings were used. The increased tension of these (and other) strings was some-times too much for the thin necks of the 4001, resulting in bowed necks and unplayable action.

"Skunk stripe"

Additional efforts were made to increase the strength of the neck. In early 1972, the neck assembly was redesigned. The wood plank was cut in two and glued to a central strip of shedua. This three-piece construction naturally resisted bending and warping. The headstock morphed into a shorter, chunkier shape with smaller "head wings" now made from maple. Typically, light-weight Grover Slimline tuners were installed, first with

The Jam's Paul Weller (left) with a Rickenbacker 330 and Bruce Foxton with one of his 4001 basses. Another sits on a stand in the background. Photo by Eileen Colton.

flat keys and later with "wavy" keys. The "skunk stripe" necks remained a feature of the 4001 until the end of production in the early 1980s.

High-gain pickups

A new pickup was developed around 1968 and installed in place of the venerable Horseshoe. The new "High-gain" pickup was more efficient and lighter in weight, as it had no need of the heavy horseshoe magnets. In place of the magnets, Rickenbacker installed a "faux horseshoe" cover, preserving the appearance of the original Horseshoe and the utility of a rest for the picking hand. It also helped shield the pickup from electronic interference. Initial covers may have been made from metal, but a plated plastic cover quickly became standard.

Also around 1968, Rickenbacker's novel "Rick-O-Sound" wiring and output became a standard feature of the 4001 bass (it had been available as a special-order option) and allowed for the signal of the two pickups to be split and sent to two different amplifiers to produce two different sounds in unison.

Trimming down

More cosmetic changes were in store in 1973. That spring, the difficult-to-install crushed-pearl inlays were replaced first by plain white inlays, then by pearlescent resin poured into routes cut in the fingerboard. As these routes did not span the fingerboard, they helped stengthen the neck. In the summer, Rickenbacker did away with the expensive and laborious checker binding, leaving only the outer binding strip.

It wasn't until late 1973 that a version of the High-gain pickup replaced the Toaster-top at the neck position. The pickup was similar to the one at the bridge position, only needing a different mounting system to fit the pick guard. The pairing of High-gain pickups remained the standard for 4001 production through the design's lifespan.

The cast-aluminum tailpiece was next, replaced by a re-engineered cast-zinc design in 1974. It used five screws instead of three to mount to the body, and lacked the gap in the middle tooth of the mute cover.

In 1975, the neck pickup was relocated a half inch farther from the fingerboard to take advantage of a harmonic node there.

The mysterious 21-fretters

Nowhere in Rickenbacker catalogs or price lists is there a mention of 4001 basses made with 21-fret fingerboards. Yet from 1969 to '71, an unknown number of them were made this way. It is not clear if they resulted from special orders or were simply experiments. It is a mystery as to how a customer could order

A rare pair of dark Burgundy and bright Fireglo 21-fret 4001 basses from 1971. 21-fretters have three frets beyond the last position marker; 20-fretters have two. Also, to maintain the scale, the tailpiece/bridge assembly was moved higher on the body. Photo by Kevin Teed.

4001 (early production) Identifying Features

Nickel-plated "reverse" Kluson tuners were the standard fit on early production 4001 basses.

Early 4001 position markers were made from white lacquer swirled in clear resin.

Rickenbacker's distinctive tailpiece/bridge/mute assembly made its debut on the new 4001. Note gap in middle "tooth" of mute cover produced by the aluminum casting process.

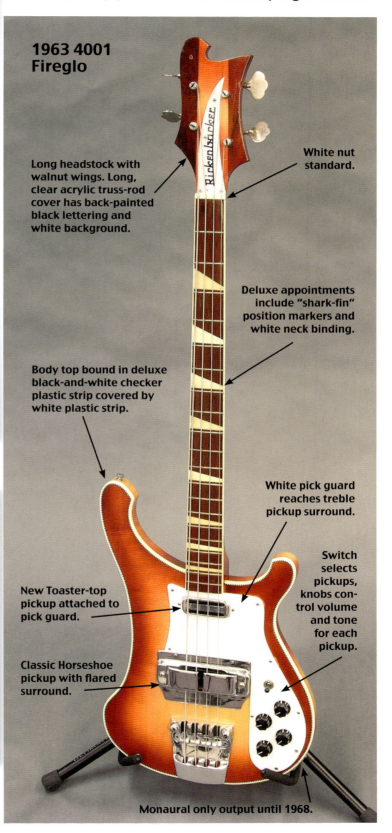

1963 4001 Fireglo

Long headstock with walnut wings. Long, clear acrylic truss-rod cover has back-painted black lettering and white background.

White nut standard.

Deluxe appointments include "shark-fin" position markers and white neck binding.

Body top bound in deluxe black-and-white checker plastic strip covered by white plastic strip.

White pick guard reaches treble pickup surround.

New Toaster-top pickup attached to pick guard.

Switch selects pickups, knobs control volume and tone for each pickup.

Classic Horseshoe pickup with flared surround.

Monaural only output until 1968.

one, and it is likely that 21-fretters were mixed in with batches of standard 20-fretters for sale.

The addition of a 21st fret allowed the player to embrace three full octaves. They can be identified by the longer neck, placing the nut about ½" farther from the body. To retain the 33¼" scale, the tailpiece/bridge assembly was correspondingly placed closer to the neck. The 21-fretters appeared in Mapleglo, Fireglo, and Burgundy, and at least one left-handed example is known to exist. They are now highly sought by collectors.

Standard production

The gradual trim changes of the early '70s settled down, but the inventory of Grover tuners was mixed with nickel-plated Kluson units. Grovers continued to appear, even on early 4003 models, in the 1980s.

Certain finishes were paired with black strip binding on the body, but always with white binding on the neck. These were usually accompanied by a black pick guard, along with an optional truss-rod cover with white lettering and black background painted on the back of a clear acrylic material.

In the mid-'70s, Rickenbacker introduced a new injection-molded truss-rod cover made in opaque plastic with raised lettering. It was usually molded in white plastic with the lettering painted black. The mold was shaped so that the cover would fit most of Rickenbacker's basses and guitars. The molded unit also allowed for other colors

(Above) This July 1965 Fireglo 4001 belonged to Stu Cook of Creedence Clearwater Revival. It was featured on the cover of the "Bayou Country" album and modified with a "jazz" pickup and custom pickup mount. Photo by Rock Stars Guitars. (Right) Deep Purple's Roger Glover blows the smoke off the water with his restored 1971 Jetglo Rickenbacker 4001. This 2007 photo was taken by Daniele Purrone.

of plastic, so black ones with white raised letters were easily produced. No raised-letter mold was made for left-handed instruments, so truss-rod covers for lefties continued to be made from back-painted clear acrylic.

Popularity

As more and more performers and recording artists played Rickenbacker basses in the 1970s, their popularity made the 4001 bass a top-seller among Rickenbacker's instruments. While the early British Invasion bassists used 4001S models, later ones were drawn to the deluxe 4001. The distinctive growl of Roger Glover's Rick (right) is evident in Deep Purple's classic "Machine Head" album, topped by the megahit "Smoke On The Water," and the driving "Highway Star." Other 4001 artists in the 1970s include Chris Squire of Yes (although his prime instrument is a 4001S/RM 1999, he also used a 21-fret 4001), Stu Cook of Credence Clearwater Revival (his 4001 above), Geddy Lee of Rush, Tiran Porter of the Doobie Brothers, Bruce Foxton of The Jam, Randy Meisner of

The Rickenbacker Electric Bass — 50 Years as Rock's Bottom

the Eagles, Martin Turner of Wishbone Ash, Dave Meros of Spock's Beard, and Jon Camp of Renaissance. Paul Goddard lent southerly soulful bass lines to the Atlanta Rhythm Section, and Phil Lynott of Thin Lizzy announced that the boys were back in town with a 4001.

Going into the 1980s, the outlandishly funky Rick James sported a White 4001, Cliff Burton banged heads with Metallica and his Burgundy 4001, and Chris Brubeck grooved a fretless Mapleglo 4001 with his group Triple Play.

Star players: (Left) Once owned by Dave Meros of Spock's Beard, this restored 1980 4001 retains Dave's custom pickguard and truss-rod cover. (Above) Jon Camp of Renaissance played this 1974 white 4001. The treble pickup was replaced with a DiMarzio Model P, a 21st fret was added, and the face of the headstock was refinished.

4001 (mid-production) Identifying Features

Closed-back Grover tuners were the norm on 4001 basses in the 1970s. This one has "wavy" keys.

Full-width crushed-pearl inlays graced the fingerboards of 4001 basses from 1964 to early 1973.

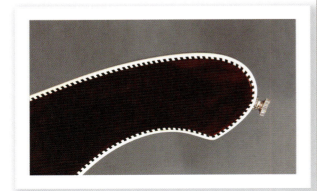

A strip of checker binding inside white binding was a hallmark of the 4001 until mid-1973.

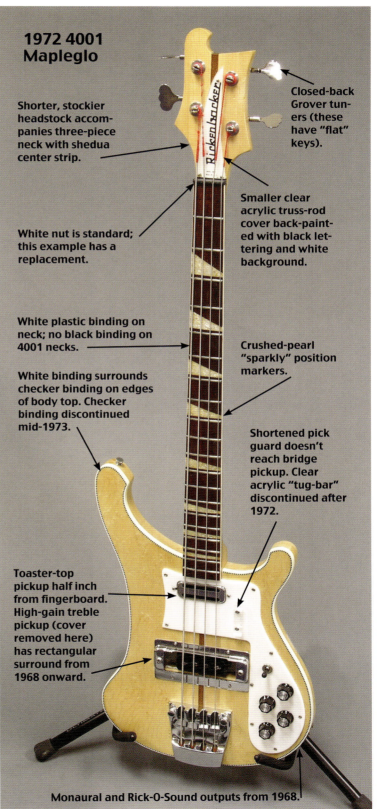

1972 4001 Mapleglo

Shorter, stockier headstock accompanies three-piece neck with shedua center strip.

Closed-back Grover tuners (these have "flat" keys).

Smaller clear acrylic truss-rod cover back-painted with black lettering and white background.

White nut is standard; this example has a replacement.

White plastic binding on neck; no black binding on 4001 necks.

Crushed-pearl "sparkly" position markers.

White binding surrounds checker binding on edges of body top. Checker binding discontinued mid-1973.

Shortened pick guard doesn't reach bridge pickup. Clear acrylic "tug-bar" discontinued after 1972.

Toaster-top pickup half inch from fingerboard. High-gain treble pickup (cover removed here) has rectangular surround from 1968 onward.

Monaural and Rick-O-Sound outputs from 1968.

The Rickenbacker Electric Bass — 50 Years as Rock's Bottom

Lefties all. Rickenbacker made lefty 4001 basses with the stock neck-through-body central assembly. Lefty truss-rod covers were back-painted clear acrylic with "smiley" lettering so that the brand would read right-side-up in the playing position. Lefty 4001 basses from the 1960s are extremely rare. (Left) This restored 1969 Fireglo 4001LH displays walnut head wings. (Center) A 1972 Mapleglo 4001LH shows the shedua center strip often called the "skunk stripe." (Right) A restored 1972 is refinished in dark Burgundy, often called "Eggplantglo" by collectors.

Old classic 4001 basses don't fade away as contemporary players have discovered. (Right) Jack Lawrence of the Raconteurs plays a late-1970s Mapleglo 4001. Josh Withers photo.

(Left) Chris Dekker of the Dutch band La La Lies plays a January 1973 Mapleglo. Photo by Irwan Notosoetarso of Fotono Photography.

(Above) Chris Brubeck plays his fretless 4001FL with his band Triple Play. His bass has an extra-wide central strip in the neck-through assembly. Photo by Rudy Lu. (Left) A beautiful 1972 Fireglo 4001FL.

The end of the beginning

Even with constant design improvements, the Rickenbacker 4001 deluxe bass was having some trouble coping with the high tension of the ever more popular round-wound strings. Rickenbacker developed a new way to adjust the necks to compensate for the extra tension, and it was decided to give the new improved bass a new model number. Production of the 4001 officially ended in 1980 with the introduction of the 4003. But Rickenbacker continued to advertise and sell the 4001 for several more years until the inventory was depleted.

4001 (late production) Identifying Features

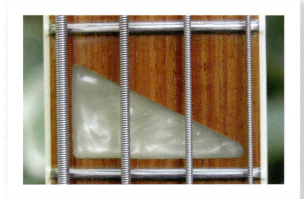

Left-handed 4001 basses featured back-painted clear acrylic truss-rod covers. Black ones are rare.

Position markers from mid-1973 are pearlescent resin poured into routed depressions in fingerboard.

Three-piece neck-through-body central planks with shedua strip were standard from mid-1972 to the end of production in the early 1980s.

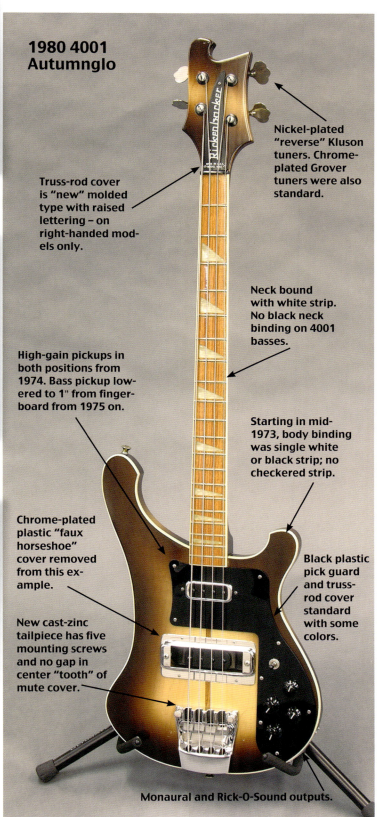

1980 4001 Autumnglo

Nickel-plated "reverse" Kluson tuners. Chrome-plated Grover tuners were also standard.

Truss-rod cover is "new" molded type with raised lettering – on right-handed models only.

Neck bound with white strip. No black neck binding on 4001 basses.

High-gain pickups in both positions from 1974. Bass pickup lowered to 1" from fingerboard from 1975 on.

Starting in mid-1973, body binding was single white or black strip; no checkered strip.

Chrome-plated plastic "faux horseshoe" cover removed from this example.

New cast-zinc tailpiece has five mounting screws and no gap in center "tooth" of mute cover.

Black plastic pick guard and truss-rod cover standard with some colors.

Monaural and Rick-O-Sound outputs.

Probably the only lefty 21-fret 4001 made, this 1971 beauty is in Mapleglo. Photo by Ian D. Martin via Peter Levett.

Gorgeous vintage Rickenbacker 4001 basses in the three classic "evergreen" colors. (Left) Deluxe appointments shine on this fine Fire-glo from 1967. Photo by Teresa Nemr & Mark Mendoza via Tony Matura.

Rounding out the trio, a 1972 Jetglo 4001 in pristine condition. Photo by Dan Machnik via Bill Henshell.

4001S Stage and studio star

1964 – 1984

Chris Squire has been playing this Rickenbacker since 1964 when he bought it at employee discount from the Boosey & Hawkes store in London where he worked. Originally Fireglo, it's undergone several repairs and refinishes over the decades. Robin Kauffman photo.

The 4001S was another natural development of the 4000 bass. It retained the basic trim of the post-1962 single-pickup bass – unbound body and neck, simple pearlescent dot position markers – but had the Toaster-top pickup and additional controls. Indeed, early factory records show that this model was sometimes referred to as the "4000+1." Later "4001S" (the "S" for "special") became the appellation for this somewhat plain-looking bass.

Looks aside, it quickly became the most famous and familiar Rickenbacker bass model in the mid-1960s because it was played by many stars of rock and roll's British Invasion.

Rose Morris 1999

Rickenbacker received a large order for guitars and basses from London's Rose Morris, the prime outlet for Rickenbacker instruments for much of Europe. There, young rockers of the mid to late '60s, having seen their heroes John Lennon, George Harrison, and then Paul McCartney using Rickenbacker instruments, just had to get their own Ricks.

Rose Morris' original order encompassed one bass and four guitar models, all finished in Fireglo, with unbound bodies and necks and simple dot position markers on the

(Text continues p.36)

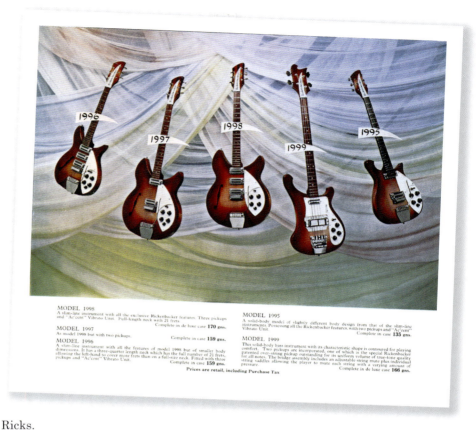

(Above) An illustrated price list for Rose Morris' selection of Rickenbacker guitars and bass. RIC archives.

Chris Squire

No bassist – not even Paul McCartney – is more closely associated with a Rickenbacker bass than Chris Squire of Yes. Squire has made a RM1999 (4001S) his principal instrument for nearly 50 years!

In a 2012 phone interview, Squire told the author how he became acquainted with his Rick back in 1964:

"I had a cheap Italian Futurama bass that my Mom bought for me; it wasn't very good. I left school early and took a job at Boosey & Hawkes, a London music store that sold classical instruments. Another branch of the store had taken delivery of imported Rickenbackers from Rose-Morris and among the instruments were three basses. Two of them were quickly bought up, one by John Entwistle (of the Who), and one by Pete Quaife (of the Kinks). I liked the look of the Rickenbacker, and after I heard Entwistle play his, I arranged to purchase the last one with my employee discount.

"It was originally that red sunburst color (Fireglo), but I dressed it up with flowery appliqués and then a silver metallic adhesive paper with white borders. I got bored with that and took it to a refinisher (Sam Lee) who sanded it down and painted it in the cream color that is still on it today. I broke the neck and had it repaired."

According to John Hall, Squire's RM1999 (4001S, serial DC127) had come into the factory for service also. The factory reconnected the treble (bridge) pickup and discovered that the previous neck repair had also glued the adjustable truss rods in place. This was rectified, a new fingerboard and frets were installed, and the bass was restored to top condition.

"I've had the same guitar tech for years now, and he makes sure it's in top running form," says Squire. "I'd feel very upset if something should ever happen to it. I grew up with it!"

Squire's main Rick inspired Rickenbacker to produce the 4001CS Chris Squire Signature Edition (p. 94).

Squire had at least two other Rick basses in his arsenal over the years. "I had one of the two 4001 eight-string prototypes; Entwistle had the other" (p. 52) "and a blonde (Mapleglo) 21-fret 4001. Both belong to a collector friend now."

Paul McCartney's Rickenbacker 4001S, DA23, as it appears today. Outline Press Ltd.

Paul McCartney

Paul McCartney is the most famous of all Rickenbacker bass players. Rickenbacker President F.C. Hall recognized a fantastic marketing opportunity and arranged to meet the Beatles in New York City as they prepared for their appearances on the Ed Sullivan Show in February 1964. Hall brought with him a new Fireglo 360-12 12-string guitar (the second one made) for George Harrison and a lefty Fireglo 4001S (perhaps the first lefty Rickenbacker bass) for McCartney. The next week, Hall had a new, slimmer Jetglo 325 sent to Miami for Lennon. While Lennon and Harrison readily accepted the new guitars, McCartney declined. Hall returned to California with the bass but didn't quit. He wrote to the Beatles' manager, Brian Epstein, encouraging him to have McCartney try the bass on their next visit to the States.

A Radio and Television Equipment Co. invoice dated January 23, 1964, lists this bass (along with three amplifiers) as being issued on a verbal order to F.C. Hall. The bass is described: "4000+1 pickup Fire left-handed DA23." Translated: 4000+1 indicates the down-trimmed 4000 bass with one pickup added – in essence, a 4001S; Fire was short for Fireglo; and DA23 is the serial number dating its manufacture to January 1964.

F.C. Hall's effort to get McCartney on the Rickenbacker bandwagon yielded results when Hall, along with son and future Rickenbacker CEO John, delivered DA23 during the Beatles' visit to Los Angeles in August 1965. McCartney accepted the bass this time and began using it in recording the "Rubber Soul" album that autumn. It appears that McCartney did not perform with the Rickenbacker on tour, although photos show the 4001S stowed behind amplifiers onstage as a backup.

McCartney's Rick on record
McCartney continued to prefer the Rickenbacker for recordings after the Beatles stopped touring, and the instrument's characteristic tones are recognizable on "Sgt. Pepper's Lonely Hearts Club Band" and other tunes from the late 1960s. The instrument appeared in the pre-music-video films of "Hello, Goodbye" and "All You Need Is Love," and in the feature film "Magical Mystery Tour." By then, each of the Beatles had personally decorated some of their instruments, and the front of the 4001S had received a drippy, psychedelic paint job of white, silver, and red on top of the original Fireglo finish.

McCartney tired of the bizarre paint job a year or so later and sanded all the finish from the bass. McCartney's Rick became his main bass during his years touring and recording with Wings. At some point in the early 1970s, he sanded the bass further, rounding off the "crested wave" shapes of the body wings.

In the mid-'70s, the 4001S was sent to Rickenbacker for service. The folks at the factory gingerly handled the iconic instrument, even though McCartney had not. They cleaned and treated the wood, replaced the dead treble (bridge) pickup, pickup surround, and cracked pickguard. Later, a "zero fret" was added below the nut by New York's Mandolin Brothers. McCartney still owns DA23.

Not the only one
A few other Rickenbacker basses have found their way into McCartney's hands. He has been photographed with a lefty mid-'70s Mapleglo fretless 4001, but little is known about this instrument. Rickenbacker CEO John Hall reported that he gifted McCartney with a prototype lefty 4004C Cheyenne bass in 1992. There is also a photo of McCartney posing with a lefty five-string Rickenbacker 4003SPC Blackstar. It is not clear whether he used any of these Rickenbackers onstage or in the studio.

Sir Paul McCartney with Wings showing the 4001S after it was stripped and the body horns rounded off. Jim Summaria photo.

fingerboards. Later, a 12-string guitar and a version of the hollow-body 4005 bass were added to the RM line. Instead of using Rickenbacker's model numbers, Rose Morris applied its own with the 4001S bass being known simply as "1999." Evidence suggests that a few RM 1999 basses were finished in Mapleglo in 1967.

New English bands quickly employed the 1999 in recordings and stage performances, most notably the Kinks' Pete Quaife, the Who's John Entwistle, and Yes's Chris Squire. Others included Maurice Gibb of the Bee Gees, Roger Waters of Pink Floyd, and Donovan (Leitch).

It appears that most 4001S basses made in the mid-1960s were sold through Rose Morris. These are now highly valued by collectors, especially when their provenance can be documented. Maurice Gibb's RM 1999 (serial DH163) was repainted white midway through the Bee Gee's music career, and eventually found its way through several collectors. This author was fortunate to have photographed it for this book in 2009.

Collectors debate whether all 4001S models from the mid-'60s should be considered RM 1999 models, but it is likely some were retained and made available to players in the U.S. The bass offered to Paul McCartney, for example, was never sent to Rose Morris. In reality, the difference between a '60s 4001S and a RM 1999 is the serial number and a boat ride.

The early 4001S/RM 1999 served as the model for Rickenbacker's successful 4001V63 (p.80) and 4001C64 (p.118) models.

Into the '70s

The 4001S was not mentioned in Rickenbacker's price lists until 1981, although it was available for special order anytime. It is likely that 4001S models made in the 1960s were simply 4000 models bored out for the installation of the second pickup and wiring. By 1973, the 4001S and single-pickup 4000 shared a common chassis with a two-piece slab body and set "three-piece" neck with its center shedua strip. Like the 4001 basses of the time, upgrades to the 4001S included High-gain pickups, newer cast-zinc tailpieces, and a variety of Kluson, Grover, and Schaller tuners. At least one fretless 4001S was made.

The end of the 4001S paralleled that of the deluxe 4001 in the early 1980s. The S model was superseded by the 4003S on the 1982 price list, but a few stragglers were sold by the factory as late as 1986.

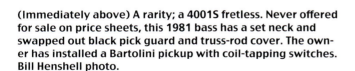

(Immediately above) A rarity; a 4001S fretless. Never offered for sale on price sheets, this 1981 bass has a set neck and swapped out black pick guard and truss-rod cover. The owner has installed a Bartolini pickup with coil-tapping switches. Bill Henshell photo.

(Top) A pair of gorgeous RM 1999s in the Australian sunshine. Rose Morris distributed Rickenbackers down under as well as in the U.K. Photos by John Alekna (left) and Darren Trott.

(Left) The late Maurice Gibb of the Bee Gees had his once-Fireglo Rose Morris 1999 refiished in White. Gibb also had a White 4001 bass with the deluxe trim and binding. (Above) A 1981 set-neck 4001S refinished in satin black with a black pick guard.

4001S/RM1999 Identifying Features

The 1960s 4001S (and therefore the Rose Morris 1999s) had the long headstock with walnut wings. The truss-rod cover was backpainted clear acrylic. Note the small ferrules for the tuning posts. John Alekna photos.

A closer look at the classic Toaster-top and Horseshoe pickups of a 1964 Rose Morris 1999 in Australia. Acrylic tug-bar has been removed from this example.

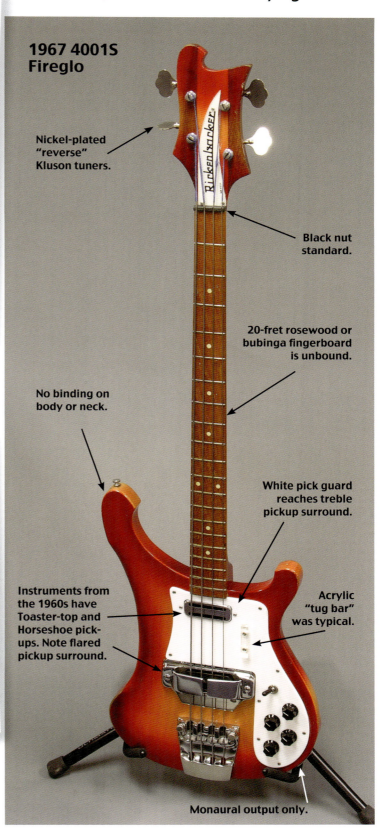

1967 4001S Fireglo

Nickel-plated "reverse" Kluson tuners.

Black nut standard.

20-fret rosewood or bubinga fingerboard is unbound.

No binding on body or neck.

White pick guard reaches treble pickup surround.

Instruments from the 1960s have Toaster-top and Horseshoe pick-ups. Note flared pickup surround.

Acrylic "tug bar" was typical.

Monaural output only.

The 4005 Family

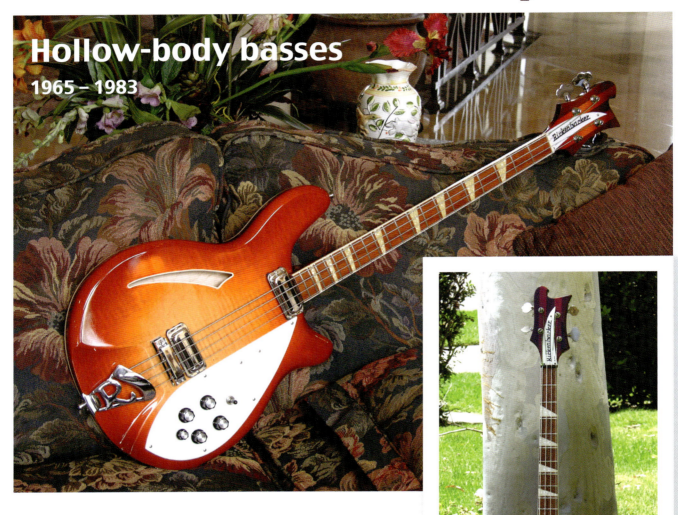

Hollow-body basses
1965 – 1983

During the 1960s and into the '70s, the hollow body 4005 was Rickenbacker's "other" bass model. While the fingerboard and headstock were like those on the classic 4001, the rest of the instrument took styling cues from the familiar new-style 360 guitar series with its rounded-top, hollow-body contours.

The neck was similar to that of the 4001, with the 33¼" scale and 20 frets, but instead of the neck-through design of the solid body basses, the 4005 featured a set neck glued into a pocket in the body. Originally, two Toaster-top pickups were mounted to the surface of the body. But these were replaced by High-gain pickups in the mid-1970s. Rather than use the standard tailpiece/bridge/mute assembly, the 4005 employed a simple bridge mounted to the body, and the string ends were anchored by Rickenbacker's "R" tailpiece over a contoured ramp.

The controls were set up similarly to those of the 360 guitar, with volume and tone pots for each pickup. The addition of a fifth "blend"

(Above) Luthier Paul Wilczynski's recreation of the classic '60s 4005 in vivid Fireglo. **(Right)** A beautiful 1967 example in deep Burgundy.

knob allowed for quick mixing of the response from the pickups. Controls and a three-way pickup selector switch (bass/both/treble) were mounted to a white acrylic pick guard covering an aperture in the hollow body. Some 4005 basses have the "Rick-O-Sound" wiring and dual outputs; some have only the monaural output.

The typical 4005 featured a top with rounded edges and a flat back with checker inner binding and white outer binding. The checker strip was dropped in mid-1973. The neck was a three-piece assembly with a wide walnut core flanked by maple sides. The 1960s 4005 basses also had walnut head wings and crushed-pearl shark fin position markers on the fingerboard. In the 1970s, the fingerboard featured poured inlays; the neck had a narrow central shedua strip, and the walnut wings were changed to maple on a stockier head.

Bound to be different

Rickenbacker also offered a double-bound variant of the 4005 bass. These featured a top with cornered edges and white strip binding on both sides of the body (above). Checker binding was not used on either side. The double-bound 4005 was sometimes coded "WB" (with binding), or "WBBS" (with binding both sides), or "OS" (old style) on order forms. Both the standard and WB versions of the 4005 were in production from 1965 to 1983, but were never as popular as the solid-body basses.

The RM 3261

In 1967, Rickenbacker delivered a number of 4005 basses to Rose Morris for distribution to European cus-

tomers. As with the 4001S, Rose Morris applied its own model number to this bass: RM 3261. It differed from the stock, rounded-top 4005 only in having an "F hole" instead of the cat's-eye opening in the top (above).

The 4005/6

The 4005 served as a baseboard for some interesting variations. The first of these was the six-string 4005/6. Similar in purpose to Fender's "Fender VI," the instrument was strung EADGBE, but an octave lower than a standard guitar. Both rounded-top and WB versions of the 4005/6 exist, and at least one lefty 4005/6 was made. While the six-string bass was offered on price lists from 1967 to '78, very few were made.

(Above) 4005 basses are rare, 4005/6 are rarer, so you can imagine how extraordinary this lefty 4005/6 must be! It's being examined by David Jenkins of True Tone Music. (Left and below) A beautiful example of a rare 4005/6 six-string bass and a closeup of the six-tuner head. Ed Hoffer photos.

A double-bound Mapleglo 4005/8 in perfect condition. The inset (right) shows the tuner arrangement on the "potato head." The large tuners were "reversed" nickle-plated Klusons, the smaller ones for the octave strings were double-line Kluson Deluxe tuners. Oyama Katsuyuki photos. (Far right) A round-top 4005/8 in Fireglo.

The 4005/8

Perhaps to offer an alternative to the 1966 Hagström H8 eight-string bass, Rickenbacker's 4005/8 saw limited production in 1967. Each bass string (EADG) was coupled with a guitar-gauge string tuned an octave higher. The 4005/8 had an unusual headstock design to ease access to the four large and four small tuning keys. Its amoeba-like shape has come to be known as "potato head" among collectors. Both rounded top and WB eight-stringers have surfaced.

Only five 4005LS were made, probably all finished in Burgundy or Jetglo. The small knob by the tailpiece controlled the light circuit. Power supply for the lights plugged into the socket next to the jackplate. This example poses in front of a trapezoidal Rickenbacker Transonic amp. Inset shows what's going on inside. Each side of the cover has a swirled-pattern layer and a clear acrylic top. Oyama Katsuyuki photos.

4005LS Light Show

Perhaps the wildest variant of the 4005 (or any brand's bass guitar) was Rickenbacker's "Light Show" bass. Accompanying the 331LS Light Show guitar, the 4005LS had an open top covered with swirly pearly translucent acrylic plastic. Mounted to a circuit board inside the body were several small electric light bulbs connected to a DC transformer through a special socket near the jackplate. The lights were wired to a circuit with the pickups so that when certain notes were played, individual bulbs would light up, creating a light show along with the sound. Crazy, man.

It was a wild (and expensive) idea, and according to John Hall, only five 4005 Light Shows were made. The earliest was built in 1967, as RIC CEO John Hall recalls accompanying his father, F.C. Hall, as he delivered a 4005LS to the Jefferson Airplane that year. Apparently, another was passed from the Byrds to John Entwistle, and another was used by the Kimberly Diamonds, a showgirl band in Las Vegas. At least one went through a major rebuild. The example here has a 1968 date stamp on the jackplate, but has post-1972 neck, pickups, and tuners.

John Entwistle's 4005

"A Rickenbacker!" shouted 13-year-old Simon Mole as he and three friends viewed a videotape of The Who's *The Kids Are Alright* film in 1979. "My mates and I pitched in to buy the tape, then had to wait two months until some-one's parents bought a video-tape player! Twenty minutes into the film the bass appeared in a black-and-white clip from '69. But as the camera panned down from the bass's headstock, the hollow body came into view and all present said I was wrong; no one had ever seen a Rick like that. I found out what a 4005 was many years later."

John Entwistle died in 2002, and his extensive bass and guitar collection was sold at auction by Sotheby's in May 2003. Mole, now a prominent Rickenbacker collector and player, attended the auction's preview day. "I had a chat with Jimmy Page (Led Zeppelin) and told him the story of how that bass had made an impression on me. He graciously autographed my London Underground map with: 'Simon, good luck with the bass – Jimmy Page.' I went home that evening and showed the autograph to my wife and said 'Led Zeppelin told me I must have the 4005 no matter the cost, and here's the proof!' I don't recall her response, but I ended up taking John Entwistle's 4005 home with me a few days later!"

Simon Mole with the 4005 bass from the John Entwistle collection. In his hand is a message from Led Zeppelin's Jimmy Page. Jonathan Mole photo.

A five-spot of "fives." (Center) Not many 4005 basses were finished in Walnut like this 1981 round-top example. Karin van de Wiel Photography via Bert Heitling. (Upper left) This 1979 round-top has an unusually dark version of Azureglo and earlier Toaster-top pickups. (Upper right) A 1967 WB in Jetglo with replacement tuners. (Lower left) A 1966 WB in Fireglo. (Lower right) Another WB, this time a 1982 in rich Burgundy.

4005 Identifying Features

Head shots: (Above) A '67 Fireglo 4005 shows the wide walnut center stripe and headwings, back-painted acrylic truss-rod cover, and nickel-plated Kluson tuners. (Below) A '79 Mapleglo 4005 has the stockier head with molded truss-rod cover and chromed Schaller tuners. Jeff Thomas photo.

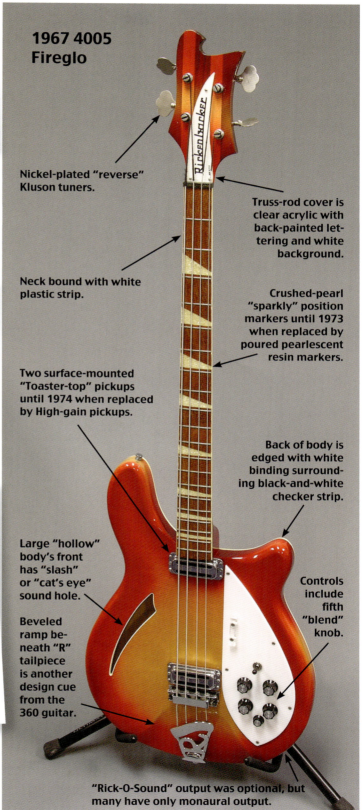

1967 4005 Fireglo

Nickel-plated "reverse" Kluson tuners.

Neck bound with white plastic strip.

Two surface-mounted "Toaster-top" pickups until 1974 when replaced by High-gain pickups.

Large "hollow" body's front has "slash" or "cat's eye" sound hole.

Beveled ramp beneath "R" tailpiece is another design cue from the 360 guitar.

Truss-rod cover is clear acrylic with back-painted lettering and white background.

Crushed-pearl "sparkly" position markers until 1973 when replaced by poured pearlescent resin markers.

Back of body is edged with white binding surrounding black-and-white checker strip.

Controls include fifth "blend" knob.

"Rick-O-Sound" output was optional, but many have only monaural output.

All 4005 basses had a "set neck" glued into a pocket in the body. This 1979 example shows the shedua strip in the center of the neck, and simple white binding that replaced the checker binding in 1973. Jeff Thomas photo.

3000 and 3001

Rickenbacker's entry-level basses

1975 – 1984

A short-scale Rickenbacker 3000 in Jetglo and a long-scale 3001 in Mapleglo rest against a vintage VOX speaker cabinet in the Phoenix, Arizona sun. John Minutaglio photo.

Any salesman knows that you can sell only so many deluxe widgets. If you also have a lower-priced widget, you can sell a lot more widgets overall. So why not develop a couple of low-cost, no-frills basses that share the quality and reliability of the trusty Rickenbacker brand?

Looking nothing like previous Rickenbacker basses, the short-scale (30") 3000 and long-scale (33¼") 3001 were developed in the early 1970s. Also unlike earlier Rickenbackers, the 3000 series utilized "bolt-on" necks – actually, the necks are attached to the bodies with wood screws.

Production

The factory had produced at least one short-scale prototype by 1971, and both the 3000 and 3001 were mentioned in the 1971 price list but missing from the lists for the next five years. It appears that production of both models was put off until late 1975; they reappeared in the 1976 price list. The short-scale 3000 cost about two thirds (the full-scale 3001 about three quarters) of the price of the flagship 4001 bass at the time of introduction.

The 3000-series basses were kept simple. Along with the bolt-on neck, each had a single High-gain pickup and monaural output. Tuning keys were the nickel-plated Klusons, and the five-screw tailpiece/bridge/mute casting of the 4000 series basses was standard. Neither body nor neck was bound, and fingerboard position markers were simple pearlescent dot inlays.

Think small

The short-scale 3000 had its output jack on the face of the pick guard along with single volume and tone knobs. The pickup was attached to the pick guard, and all the electronics fit into routs in the top of the bass. The body was an assembly of two maple planks, with a pocket milled away for the neck. The neck was a single-piece plank with maple "head wings" attached. The bubinga fingerboard had 21 frets. Overall, the 3000 looked much like the 3001, but was smaller.

3000 Identifying Features

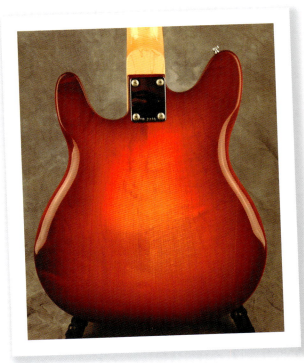

Headstock of 3000 is similar to but smaller than the head of the 3001.

The neck/body mounting plate carries the engraved serial number. Necks and headstocks were unpainted but were clear coated. Ron O'Keefe photos.

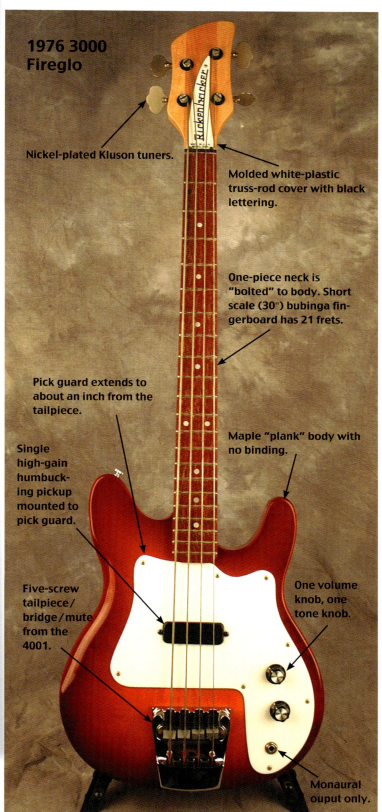

1976 3000 Fireglo

Nickel-plated Kluson tuners.

Molded white-plastic truss-rod cover with black lettering.

One-piece neck is "bolted" to body. Short scale (30") bubinga fingerboard has 21 frets.

Pick guard extends to about an inch from the tailpiece.

Maple "plank" body with no binding.

Single high-gain humbucking pickup mounted to pick guard.

Five-screw tailpiece/bridge/mute from the 4001.

One volume knob, one tone knob.

Monaural ouput only.

(Above) Bob Hardy of Franz Ferdinand plays his Walnut 3001. Tony Felgueiras photo. (Far left) There were perhaps a handful of fretless 3001s made like this Walnut beauty. Brenda Almond photo. (Right) Judging from existing examples, most 3000 and 3001 basses were made in Mapleglo and Walnut. Other colors such as Fireglo and Jetglo are uncommon, and this 1977 Azureglo 3001 can be considered rare – especially in this near perfect condition. Donald Mouck photo.

Think big

The long-scale 3001 shared shapes and overall look with the 3000, but was obviously larger – and heavier, weighing around 12 pounds. Placement of the pickup and controls was similar to that of the 3000, but the output jack was placed on the edge of the body rather than on the pick guard. Unlike the 3000, the 3001 had its tone control bifurcated into bass-cut and treble-cut potentiometers. In the catalog, these controls are described as "bass boost" and "treble boost." Tomato, tomahto: It all depends on which way you turn the knobs.

The 3001's neck was a three-piece assembly of a maple plank split by a shedua strip for added stability. It had 20 frets like most of Rickenbacker's other full-scale basses. A handful of fretless 3001 basses was made. Both models were discontinued in 1984, and the full-scale 3001 developed into the new 2030 Hamburg and 2050 El Dorado basses.

3001 Identifying Features

The 3001's neck is a three-piece maple/shedua/maple construction. Ron O'Keefe photos.

Body of 3001 bass is two-piece construction. Four wood screws fasten the neck to a pocket in the body. Chris Poteat photo.

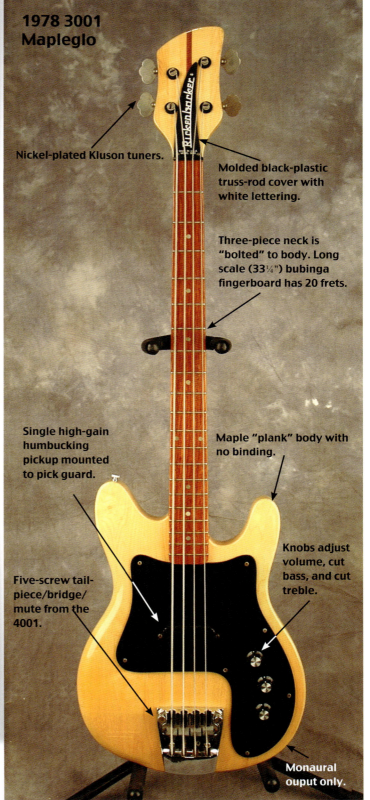

1978 3001 Mapleglo

Nickel-plated Kluson tuners.

Molded black-plastic truss-rod cover with white lettering.

Three-piece neck is "bolted" to body. Long scale (33¼") bubinga fingerboard has 20 frets.

Single high-gain humbucking pickup mounted to pick guard.

Maple "plank" body with no binding.

Knobs adjust volume, cut bass, and cut treble.

Five-screw tailpiece/bridge/mute from the 4001.

Monaural ouput only.

4008

Adding more "voice"

1975 – 1985

The 1973 "4001/8" prototype from the John Entwistle collection. Photo by Steve Pitkin, Pitkin Studio.

In the mid-1970s, Rickenbacker reintroduced the eight-string bass. The rise of "progressive rock" in that decade increased the demand for a bass with more voice which the higher-octave-string setup could provide.

Prototypes

Back in the late 1960s, a few eight-string, hollow-body 4005 basses were produced. But this time, Rickenbacker worked up an eight-string version of the flagship 4001. In the summer of 1973, two 4001 basses were built with the odd "potato head" headstock similar to that found on the 4005/8. These first "prototypes" ended up in the hands of premiere bassists Chris Squire of Yes and John Entwistle of the Who. Both basses were finished in white with checker and black body binding, white neck binding, and pearlescent dot position markers on the bubinga fingerboard. The standard tuners were interspersed with small guitar tuners for the lighter octave strings.

The cast tailpiece made room for the extra strings by having the "teeth" of the mute cover removed. An extra wood screw in the middle of the bottom end kept the tailpiece from lifting with the strain of eight strings.

The prototypes had the lighter octave strings to the right of the heavier bass strings (as viewed from straight ahead). This setup favored bassists who plucked with fingers, ensuring the lighter strings were plucked evenly. Only four saddles were installed in the bridge, one for each string pair.

Production models

The new eight-string bass differed from the prototypes in several ways, most obviously in having a new headstock design. The new shape was a stretched-out version of the standard 4001 head. Instead of the prototype's alternating tuners, the production models had eight of the new streamlined Schaller units installed.

Standard 4008 basses had an unbound body but a bound neck (a feature distinguishing it from the later, unbound-neck 4003/8). The factory continued to use the six-pole Toaster-top pickup in the neck position, with the four-pole High-gain pickup in the bridge position.

Also differing from the prototypes, the string pairs were set up with the lighter octave strings to the left, which favored pick players. Once again, the tailpiece had the teeth of the mute cover removed, but now also had one large opening in the butt end for the string routes. Two extra screws (for a total of seven) held the tailpiece down.

Although not many were made, the 4008 was available from 1975 (where it was described as "4001/8" in the March 1, 1975, price list) through 1985.

The new-style truss-rod system of the 4003 was applied to the 4008 basses made in the early 1980s. This placed the adjusting nuts of the hairpin truss rods at the body end of the channels rather than the traditional headstock end. While there are only a few examples to study, it appears that the dual "stereo" outputs of the Rick-O-Sound were standard on the production 4008. The 4008 was replaced by the 4003S/8 in 1986.

4008 Identifying Features

Eight streamlined chrome-plated Schaller tuners were placed on the nearly straight-edged head-stock. Photos by Sue Daley/Wicked Grin Photography via Eden MacKenzie.

The "teeth" of the mute cover were removed, as were the routing holes in the base of the cast tail-piece. Seven screws (three under the bridge) were needed to prevent "tail lift."

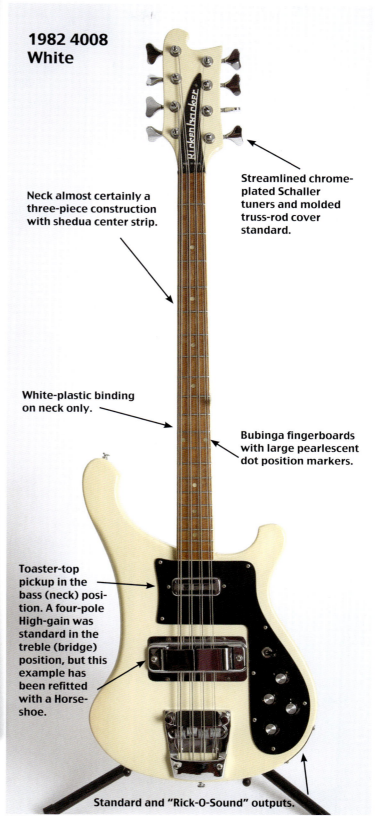

1982 4008 White

Neck almost certainly a three-piece construction with shedua center strip.

White-plastic binding on neck only.

Toaster-top pickup in the bass (neck) position. A four-pole High-gain was standard in the treble (bridge) position, but this example has been refitted with a Horse-shoe.

Streamlined chrome-plated Schaller tuners and molded truss-rod cover standard.

Bubinga fingerboards with large pearlescent dot position markers.

Standard and "Rick-O-Sound" outputs.

4080 Bass/Guitar

Rickenbacker's double-neck

1975 – 1992

Many collectors would consider the Rickenbacker 4080 to be a guitar with a bass attached, but the readers of this book know better; it's a bass with a guitar added on. There's no denying that a double-neck instrument is a showpiece, but there are some utilitarian aspects to it as well. Double-neck guitars are usually made with six- and twelve-string necks lashed together. Rickenbacker's 362/12 guitar is an example of this pairing. There are also instruments with two six-strings together, allowing for alternate tuning or for setting up one neck for slide play.

Rickenbacker's 4080 bass/guitar was introduced in 1975. The "upper" half is unmistakably a 4001 bass

(Above) Pete Trewavas of Marillion plays a White 4080/12. Linda Heath photo. A gorgeous 1981 4080 bass/six-string guitar in Walnut with white and chrome trim.

4080 Identifying Features

Tuners on most 4080s are Grover Rotomatics for the guitar headstock and Klusons for the bass.

Both necks are screwed and glued to the "double-wide" body. Bass neck is three-piece with central shedua strip.

The tailpieces are the standard castings found on the 4001 bass and 480 guitar.

1975 4080 Mapleglo

Bass is long-scale (33¼"). Bubinga fingerboard has 20 frets.

Both necks and body are bound.

All pickups are High-gain units.

These truss-rod covers are back-painted clear acrylic, but later models featured molded units with raised lettering.

Top switch selects bass or guitar. Bottom switch selects bass or treble pickups.

Knobs adjust volume and tone. Fifth knob blends the pickups.

Monaural and Rick-O-Sound outputs.

with 20 frets, while the "lower" is essentially Rickenbacker's 480 six-string guitar with 24 frets. The pair meet in the middle in one large (and heavy) body assembly to which both necks are "bolted" (wood screwed and glued, really).

The High-gain pickups and hardware of the 4080 are the same as the 4001 and 480, but wired through a single control center. A two-way toggle switch near the guitar fingerboard activates either the bass or guitar, while the toggle near the guitar bridge selects the bass (neck), treble (bridge), or both pickups of the instrument that is activated. Likewise, the knobs control volume and tone for each pickup, and a smaller fifth knob controls a "blend" of pickup response. The 4080 came standard with the company's trademarked Rick-O-Sound feature and an oversized case.

Rickenbacker also produced a number of 4080/12s with a 12-string guitar headstock similar to that on the 360/12 guitar, with additional modifications to the "R" tailpiece and bridge. Geddy Lee of Rush owned at least two 4080s and performed with them on occasion.

According to RIC price sheets the 4080 double-neck was available into 1992, but it appears that most of them were produced in the late 1970s and early '80s.

(Top left) A 1975 4080 in Azureglo with black pick guards and truss-rod covers. (Top right) A beautiful 1979 4080 in Burgundy with black pick guards and truss-rod covers. (Bottom right) A 1975 White 4080 with white plastic but black binding on the body. (Below left) This 1978 4080/12 is a gorgeous restoration. It has many custom features, including new full-width, crushed-pearl fingerboard inlays, checker binding on the body, classic Horseshoe pickup, walnut head wings, and gold back-painted pick guards and truss-rod covers.

4002 Low impedance for recording

1977 – 1984

In the mid-1970s, Rickenbacker produced a new bass designed to be used by studio musicians as well as stage performers. Sales literature of the period described the 4002 as "the finest electric bass we have ever produced." Also stating that it was a "limited-edition," the advertisements described the new features that included "super high-gain humbucking pickups" and "low-imped-

(Above) A Walnut 4002 shines in the spotlight. Dave Pascoe photo. (Right) Rickenbacker collectors Steve Wood and David McDonald show off their nearly identical Mapleglo 4002s. David McDonald photo.

ance output jack for direct connection with recording studio control board." This was accomplished with a circuit that ran out through a standard XLR ("cannon") jack. The new pickups were positioned lower on the body and were mounted to a fancy four-layer laminated pick guard. The tailpiece/bridge/mute assembly and controls were similar to those of the 4001.

Deluxe wood and trim

In addition to the new electronics, the 4002 featured deluxe birdseye or curly maple body wings and checker binding on the body, with black strip binding around it and along the neck and around the headstock. This is the only production Rickenbacker bass with a bound head-stock. The fingerboard was ebony with large pearlescent dot markers, and extended over the body to include a 21st fret.

The 4002 was available only in Mapleglo and Walnut (brown burst). Perhaps ahead of its time, the 4002 was not a big seller, and originally cost twice as much as the 4001. Likely only a few hundred were produced between 1977 and 1984. A handful of fretless 4002 basses were made. While the left-handed option was available on the 4002, lefty examples have yet to be found.

(Right) A rare and well-appreciated fretless 4002 in Walnut. GingerDawn Seaboyer photo. (Below) Three outputs define the 4002: The typical "Standard" (monaural) and "Rick-O-Sound" (stereo) outputs in company with a low-impedance XLR jack. (Below right) The insides of the 4002 show that both pickups are mounted to the pickguard. Jeff Thomas photos.

4002 Identifying Features

deluxe features include black strip ... the front, walnut "head wings," and ... ...rough the middle of the neck-through-... ...tion. Jeff Thomas photo.

Premium birdseye or "curly" maple was used for the body wings on most 4002 basses. Dave Pascoe photo.

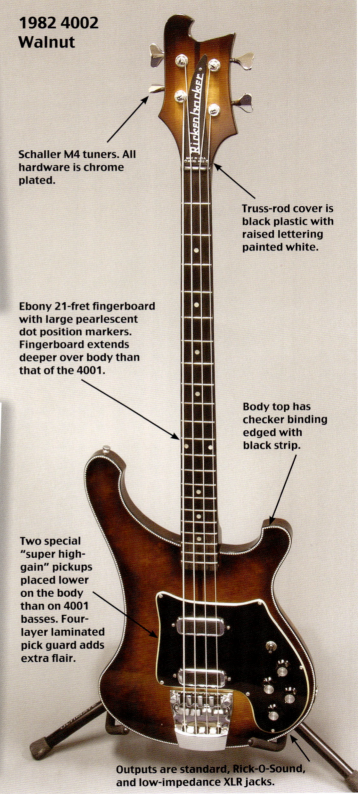

**1982 4002
Walnut**

Schaller M4 tuners. All hardware is chrome plated.

Truss-rod cover is black plastic with raised lettering painted white.

Ebony 21-fret fingerboard with large pearlescent dot position markers. Fingerboard extends deeper over body than that of the 4001.

Body top has checker binding edged with black strip.

Two special "super high-gain" pickups placed lower on the body than on 4001 basses. Four-layer laminated pick guard adds extra flair.

Outputs are standard, Rick-O-Sound, and low-impedance XLR jacks.

4003

1980 –

The ultimate flagship

Meet the new bass! Same as the old bass? Well, not quite. The 4003 replaced the 4001 as the flagship of the Rickenbacker bass fleet starting in 1980. Outwardly, there was little difference between the old and the new. In fact, the changes were no more drastic than other structural and cosmetic improvements made to the 4001 during the 1960s and '70s. Most of the production changes during those years improved electronics and hardware, and strengthened the neck to counter increased tension of the round-wound strings then in vogue.

The most obvious change to the 4003 was the structure of the neck. Although a few early 4003 basses may have been made with a three-piece neck similar to the 4001, most were made with either a two-piece or a one-piece neck. That aside, the reason for the change was the repositioning of the truss rods. The early 4003 basses used the same folded "hairpin" truss rods of the 4001, but instead of having the adjustment nuts accessed in a cavity in the headstock, they were placed with the adjusters and thrust plate at the body end of the neck, accessible in the cavity cut for the neck pickup. To improve access to the adjusters, the pick guard was split in two. By removing a few mounting screws, the player could swing the top half of the pick guard aside and insert a wrench to adjust the truss rods.

This new design was incorporated in the deluxe bass in 1980, and production of the old style ceased. It seems this structural improvement to the basic 4001 design wasn't drastic. So why did Rickenbacker change the model number? In today's world of on-demand production and minimal inventory, it probably wouldn't have been needed, but in 1980 the company held considerable numbers of old-style 4001 basses awaiting orders, yet wanted to make the new design available immediately. Company catalogs trumpeted the new 4003 bass as being designed for round-wound strings (and the higher tension they possessed at the time), and also touted the 4001 bass as suitable for "flat wound" strings. Although production of the 4001 bass ceased in 1980, the retired battlewagon was still shown in catalogs and price lists through 1985.

The folded hairpin truss rods with the adjusters at the body end were also used in the eight-string 4008 in the early 1980s, and installed in the new 4003S and 4003SB models starting in 1982.

Change is a good thing

By spring of 1986, the old 4001 (and 4000, 4001S, and 4001 fretless) basses had passed out of inventory, and the new 4003 design and model number was well established as the flagship. At this point, RIC engineers changed the truss system yet again. Instead of the hairpin truss rods, RIC substituted two straight rods resting in gently arched channels in the neck. These were threaded on both ends, with the adjusting

(Facing page) Al Cisneros of Sleep and Om plays his 2008 Fireglo 4003 bass. Tim Bugbee photo. **(Right)** An early (1982) 4003, this lefty is finished in Burgundy.

Marlon Deppen of the Seattle band Alabaster digs into his 1985 Red 4003. Katie Adams photo.

nuts now back at the head end of the neck. These new rods worked differently from the old ones, and more importantly, worked more like the rods found in most other brands of guitars and basses.

In 1985, chrome-plated, open-backed, German-made tuners became the standard, replacing the nickel-plated Kluson and chrome-plated, closed-back Grover units. The new tuners were custom-made by Schaller and featured the Rickenbacker brand recessed in the baseplate.

4003 (early production) Identifying Features

Early 4003s had the classic "hairpin" truss rods mounted with the adjustment nuts and thrust plates at the body end of the neck. Only routed channels were visible in the headstock. CJ Johansson photos.

The cluster of three screws identifies the split pick guard that was standard on the 4003 from 1980 to 1986.

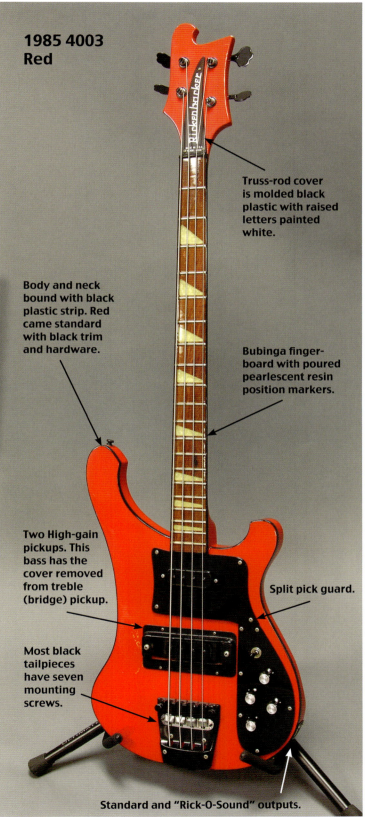

1985 4003 Red

Truss-rod cover is molded black plastic with raised letters painted white.

Body and neck bound with black plastic strip. Red came standard with black trim and hardware.

Bubinga fingerboard with poured pearlescent resin position markers.

Two High-gain pickups. This bass has the cover removed from treble (bridge) pickup.

Split pick guard.

Most black tailpieces have seven mounting screws.

Standard and "Rick-O-Sound" outputs.

Pump it up

To many players, especially those adopting the Rickenbacker bass for heavy metal music, the treble (bridge) High-gain pickup was a weakling compared with the same pickup in the bass (neck) position. Some never discovered that there was a simple solution to that "problem." From the beginning of the Rickenbacker bass design, a .0047µF (microfarad) capacitor was wired into the circuit to cut bass response from the treble pickup, giving it a brighter sound. Simply replacing the capacitor with a piece of wire was the quick and easy fix. In 1984, RIC responded to customer preferences and jettisoned the capacitor, giving the 4003 a more ballsy sound right out of the box.

Steady progress

Incremental improvements were incorporated as production of the 4003 continued. By late 1996, RIC was shaping the principal wood components of its instruments with modern "CNC" (computer-numerical control) cutting machines, and with them, consistent shapes were ensured. Through the 1980s, the width of the cresting-wave "horns" on the body wings had gradually increased. A return to the svelte horns of the 1960s and '70s was loaded into the digital templates in the CNC machines.

In late 2005, the factory brought back contrasting "wings" to the headstocks of most basses. These add a little retro vibe as they emulate the instruments from the 1960s. The head wings were made from either walnut or retified (roasted) maple.

Starting early in 2006, RIC restored the .0047µF (microfarad) bass-cut capacitor to the circuitry. But a push/pull switch offers the option to activate it. Pulling up on the bridge pickup's tone knob puts the capacitor in play, cutting the bass response for that pickup; pushing the knob back down bypasses the capacitor for increased bass response.

In fall 2006, adjustable poles became standard on the two High-gain pickups; a turn of an Allen wrench could raise or lower each pole to increase or decrease response without moving the entire pickup.

With the aid of the new CNC milling process, RIC was able to return to installing full-width inlays for position markers on the fingerboards. Recesses in the wood and pieces of pearloid plastic were computer-cut to match. This process replaced the old poured-resin inlays on the 4003 basses by early 2008.

A return to a two-piece neck-through construction was instituted in early 2009. The two-piece assembly further strengthens the neck and reduces warp and twist.

In 2010, RIC replaced its decades-old conversion-varnish finish with new, UV-cured polyester formulas that are more environmentally friendly. Under concentrated ultraviolet light, they cure in a fraction of the time it took using the old formulas.

For decades, RIC had used bubinga for nearly all of its

First in Rickenbacker's "Color of the Year" program, Sea Green graces the full-dress 4003 bass built in 2000. (Below) Amy Humphrey of the indie-rock duo Clatter totes her Jetglo 4003 through a field of goldenrod. Joe Hayes, husband and the drummer half of the duo, took the photo.

(Above) Bryce Soderberg of Lifehouse plays several Ricks on stage, including this 4003 in Blueburst. Don Henderson photo. (Left) Another 4003 bass in Blueburst, the 2005 "Color of the Year."

instruments' fingerboards. In the fall of 2011, the factory began using Caribbean rosewood, a material with similar strength and tonal qualities, but featuring more dramatic grain and "figuring." Ben Hall, RIC production manager and son of company owner, John Hall, states, "The tone is indistinguishable from bubinga, which makes sense as neither African rosewood (bubinga) nor Caribbean rosewood (chechen) are true rosewoods in the Dalbergia family. Retaining the tonal properties of bubinga was a very important consideration for us in switching to Caribbean rosewood." Chechen is more brown, compared with the rusty-red of bubinga. RIC is careful to use only farm-raised hardwoods for its instruments.

4003 (mid-production) Identifying Features

New double-threaded rods replaced the old "hair-pin" truss rods by 1986. The adjustment nuts returned to the head end of the truss rods.

Acorn nuts anchor the truss rods on the body end.

High-gain pickups have non-adjustable domed poles.

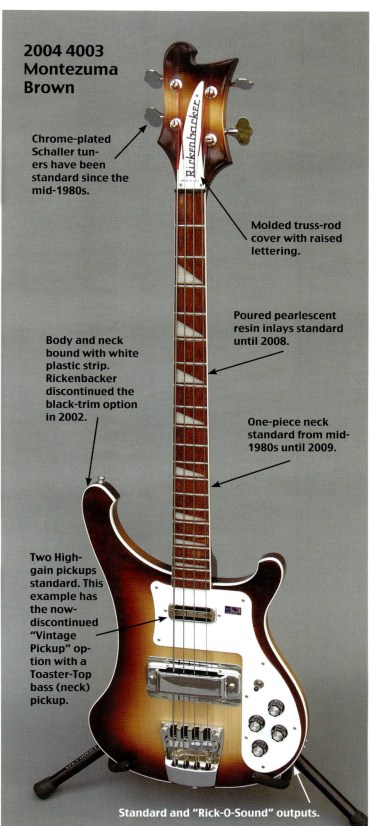

2004 4003 Montezuma Brown

Chrome-plated Schaller tuners have been standard since the mid-1980s.

Molded truss-rod cover with raised lettering.

Poured pearlescent resin inlays standard until 2008.

Body and neck bound with white plastic strip. Rickenbacker discontinued the black-trim option in 2002.

One-piece neck standard from mid-1980s until 2009.

Two High-gain pickups standard. This example has the now-discontinued "Vintage Pickup" option with a Toaster-Top bass (neck) pickup.

Standard and "Rick-O-Sound" outputs.

The "Shadow" knows

In 1986, RIC received an order from Guitar Center for a special Rickenbacker 4003 bass. This was the "Shadow." Apparently made for a special occasion, either 50 or 60 Shadows were produced. They featured a Jetglo finish, but with the addition of checker inner binding and black outer binding on the body. Instead of the traditional shark-fin inlays, the Shadow had large black dot position markers on the fingerboard. By the mid-1980s, RIC had started to produce blackened hardware (tuners, pickup surrounds, tailpiece, and strap pins), and these were added to the Shadow's scheme. The result is a particularly handsome instrument. Players also appreciated the Shadow's very thin neck.

75th Anniversary 4003

To celebrate the company's 75th anniversary in 2006, a special commemorative issue of the 4003 was produced. A special anniversary design was laser-etched into the back side of a clear acrylic pick guard, which was then back-painted in gold. Similarly a clear-acrylic truss rod cover featured the Rickenbacker lettering in silver with a gold background.

A special Dark Cherry Metallic color was chosen for the anniversary model. This deep, fine-grained metallic port-wine color perfectly contrasts the gold plastic commemorative accessories. Just 75 of the 4003 75th Anniversary were produced in 2006-07 (along with 75 each of the 330, 360, and 660 six-string guitars).

(Above) Paul Wilson of Snow Patrol plays his lefty Jetglo 4003. Steve Jennings photo. (Left) The fretless version was designated 4003FL, here in the 2006 "Color of the Year," Amber Fireglo.

Special delivery to Japan

Rickenbackers are popular in Japan, and orders from retailers there warrant special attention from the factory. In 2003, a special order was placed for 4003 basses equipped with Toaster pickups in the neck (bass) positions and old-style checker binding on the bodies. It appears that two dozen each of Fireglo and Jetglo basses were delivered.

Today's flagship

Because the Rickenbacker 4003 deluxe bass has been in constant production since 1980, and is in constant demand by players and collectors, it is safe to say that more 4003 basses have been built and sold than any other model of Rickenbacker bass – possibly more than all the other models combined.

4003 (current production) Identifying Features

Chrome-plated Schaller tuners with embossed Rickenbacker brand name are standard on 4003 basses. Bass courtesy Wade's Guitar Shop, Milwaukee, WI.

Computer cut, full-width pearlescent position markers became standard in 2008. Caribbean rosewood (chechen) replaced African rosewood (bubinga) as standard fingerboard material in late 2011.

Since late 2006, poles on both High-gain pickups can be adjusted with an Allen key.

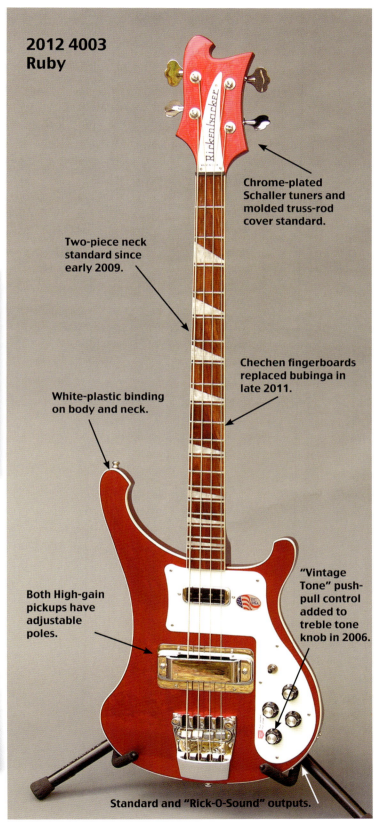

2012 4003 Ruby

Chrome-plated Schaller tuners and molded truss-rod cover standard.

Two-piece neck standard since early 2009.

Chechen fingerboards replaced bubinga in late 2011.

White-plastic binding on body and neck.

Both High-gain pickups have adjustable poles.

"Vintage Tone" push-pull control added to treble tone knob in 2006.

Standard and "Rick-O-Sound" outputs.

4001SB/4003SB
RIC's first "vintage" bass

1981 – 1983

THREE BRAND NEW,
GRAND OLD GUITARS...

By popular demand, Rickenbacker announces an encore
performance by three classics from the past. For a limited time
only, the Models 320B, 4003SB and the 360/12BWB are
available with factory installed "chrome bar" pickups and other
identifying features used in the 60's. These pickups are also
available separately and in sets for installation on other fine
Rickenbacker models. Vintage models are available in both
right and left hand versions.

"B" Series Vintage Favorites From Rickenbacker

For additional information, contact your local Rickenbacker dealer, or write to:
RICKENBACKER, INC. /Dept. 109/P.O. Box 2275/Santa Ana, CA 92707-0275

Rickenbacker sales flyer courtesy RIC Archives.

As if Rickenbacker instruments weren't "retro" enough on their own, Rickenbacker started to market classic guitars in 1981 as the "B Series Vintage Favorites." The advertisements for the "B Series" never mention the Beatles, but it was obvious that Rickenbacker was targeting Fab Four fans. The two guitars and the one bass were supposed to look like the Beatles' famous Rickenbackers.

It appears that Rickenbacker marketed the B series as early as 1981. A Japanese advertising brochure from that year highlights the "4001SB" and shows a lefty 4001S bass (distinguished by the shedua strip down the middle of the headstock but not body) with a Toaster-top pickup in the bass (neck) position. This bass (or a similar one) was used in the U.S. sales flyer as well (left), although now described as the "4003SB."

Rickenbacker likely made the first B model basses from remaining stock of 4001S. When they were gone, B models were made from the then-new 4003S with the added Toaster (described in the ad as the "chrome bar pickup"). A 4003SB can also be identified by the split pickguard with the hairpin truss rod adjusting nuts at the body end of the neck.

In either case, the similarity of the B model to Paul McCartney's well-used 4001S was superficial and not really "vintage." Shortly after buying the company in 1984, John Hall stopped production of the B model and replaced it with the more accurately "vintage" 4001V63.

4003SB Identifying Features

Gradually phased out of inventory, the streamlined Grover tuners were often fit to late 4001 and early 4003 basses. Ken Earnest photos.

The Grover tuners on this 4003SB had "wavy" keys. Neither these tuners nor the molded truss-rod cover were "vintage accurate" for an emulation of Paul McCartney's 1964 4001S bass.

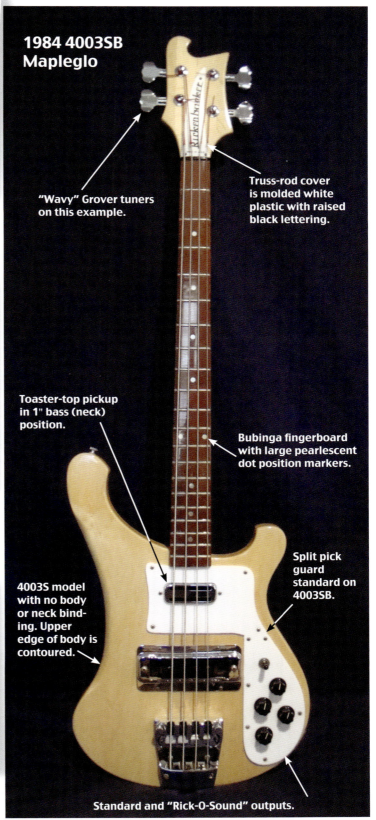

1984 4003SB Mapleglo

"Wavy" Grover tuners on this example.

Truss-rod cover is molded white plastic with raised black lettering.

Toaster-top pickup in 1" bass (neck) position.

Bubinga fingerboard with large pearlescent dot position markers.

4003S model with no body or neck binding. Upper edge of body is contoured.

Split pick guard standard on 4003SB.

Standard and "Rick-O-Sound" outputs.

Although essentially a 4003S model, this SB was fitted with both Standard and Rick-O-Sound outputs.

4003S
Back to bassics
1982 – 1996

Call it "stripped down," "basic trim," or even "low-vis," there always seems to be a call for an unbound, down-trimmed, two-pickup, solid-body bass in the Rickenbacker line. Even though the previous 4001S was minimally advertised, demand spiked in the 1960s when it was seen being played by Paul McCartney, Chris Squire, John Entwistle, Peter Quaife, Maurice Gibb, and many others. The 4003S replaced the 4001S in 1982 and, unlike its ancestor, it was prominently shown in catalog brochures and price lists.

The S model featured an unbound body and neck and pearlescent dot position markers on the fingerboard. A monaural output was standard, but a few have appeared with the dual standard and Rick-O-Sound stereo outputs.

Like the early 4003, the new 4003S featured the classic hairpin folded truss rods with the adjustment nuts placed at the body end of the neck. A two-piece pick guard facilitated access to the rod adjusters. Several early 4003 and 4003S basses were built with two-piece neck-through assemblies, while later models had one-piece neck-through units.

The 4003S bass was equipped with two High-gain pickups, the bass (neck) pickup about 1" from the neck, and the treble (bridge) pickup tucked into the large cavity near the middle of the body.

The new 4003S was first marketed on price sheets "with round-wound strings" alongside the old 4001S (for flat-wound strings). In 1982, both S models were list priced at $810, compared with $880 for the deluxe 4003 and remaining 4001 models.

Improvements

As with the deluxe 4003 model, the truss system was redesigned in early 1986 to the double-ended rods. The new rods' adjusters were now positioned at the headstock, so the split pick guard was no longer needed and the standard one-piece pick guard returned.

A handful of 4003S/FL fretless basses were made. The 4003S became the canvas for new Rickenbacker bass models to come: the five-string 4003S/5; the eight-string 4003S/8; the vintage 4003SB, 4001V63, 4001CS Chris Squire Limited Edition, and 4001C64/C64S; and the racy 4003SPC specials, all of which are highlighted in their own chapters.

By late 1995, the 4003S disappeared from official price sheets. But production extended into late 1996. By then players desiring the unbound, dot-neck appearance were redirected to the vintage models.

This early '90s 4003S in Midnight Blue is spiced up with a custom pearlescent pick guard and blue-jewel tops to the control knobs.

4003S Identifying Features

4003S basses from 1982 through 1985 had the split pick guard and the hairpin truss rods adjusted at the body end.

Here's proof that any model can be manufactured as a fretless bass. The 4003SFL was never included in official price sheets.

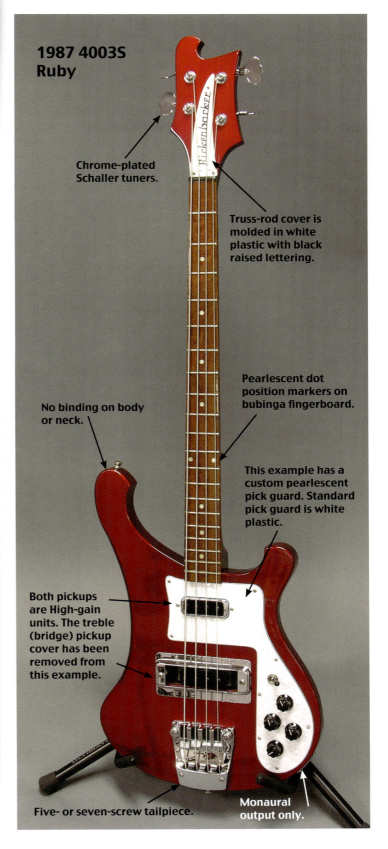

1987 4003S Ruby

Chrome-plated Schaller tuners.

Truss-rod cover is molded in white plastic with black raised lettering.

No binding on body or neck.

Pearlescent dot position markers on bubinga fingerboard.

This example has a custom pearlescent pick guard. Standard pick guard is white plastic.

Both pickups are High-gain units. The treble (bridge) pickup cover has been removed from this example.

Five- or seven-screw tailpiece.

Monaural output only.

2030 Hamburg and 2050 El Dorado

Rickenbacker goes modern

1984 – 1992

Marketed in 1985, Rickenbacker's "2000 series" basses and its accompanying "200 series" guitars were truly new. While the outline of the new bass was close to the old 3001, everything else was different. First, the one-piece "bolt-on" neck enjoyed the addition of the new, more conventional truss-rod system as used in the 4003. Another pickup was added, and along with it an additional set of volume and tone controls and a microswitch to activate either or both pickups.

Instead of the familiar Rickenbacker unit, as used on the 3000/3001, the new bass featured a Schaller tailpiece with roller bridges that could be independently raised or lowered and adjusted for intonation. However, this unit had no mute. Tuners for the 2030/2050 were also Schaller units, custom manufactured with "Rickenbacker" stamped into the base plate.

Modern circuitry

Perhaps the biggest innovation was the application of a copyrighted printed circuit board that sat in the control cavity cut into the back of the body. All the controls and the output jack were mounted to the board, so the only wires needed were the leads to the pickups and a ground wire to the bridge. Although the board was placed close to the edge of the body, a cutaway was needed to allow the cord to reach the output jack.

The modern circuit loaded into the back of the body has given some the impression that it is an "active" bass (battery-boosted signals).

A fine vintage for the 2030 Hamburg bass, finished in Ruby with a black truss-rod cover and Schaller bridge. David Pascoe photo.

(Above) A great portrait shows the evolution of Rickenbacker's alternate bass. The Mapleglo 3001 (left) and 2030 Hamburg share overall shape and "bolt-on" neck construction, but nearly everything else is new on the Hamburg. Ron O'Keefe photo. (Right) A couple of music-store finds: 2030 Hamburg basses in Silver and Red, both with blackened hardware. Jeff Rath photos.

But as there is no battery involved; the 2030/2050 basses are passive. Through 1987, RIC literature was describing this arrangement as "semi-active electronics," but this vague wording was dropped from the 1988 descriptions.

No pick guards were used, so the pickups were mounted in shallow depressions in the front of the body. Each pickup had a pair of spring-loaded fittings that accepted long Allen-headed bolts mounted in the back of the body. By turning the bolts, the player could adjust the height of the pickups.

Early 2030 and 2050 basses appeared with the pickups that were used on the 3000/3001 basses, modified to fit the new mounting system. But in time, new humbucking pickups were developed, and they were featured on most 2030s and 2050s.

Basses with names

Also for the first time, the new bass models received names: The unbound 2030 was named Hamburg, likely a

salute to the German city that was pivotal to the Beatles success; and the bound 2050 was named for the legendary "Lost City of Gold," El Dorado. The names were shared with the similar guitars in the series, the 230 Hamburg and 250 El Dorado.

Unlike the earlier 3001 and later 2020 and 2060 basses, the necks on all 2030 and 2050 basses were painted to match the color of the body, and bound with either white or black plastic strips. Hamburgs featured either chrome-plated or blackened hardware. El Dorados, in keeping with their name, featured gold-plated hardware – a first for Rickenbacker.

Molded black-plastic truss-rod covers were used on the 2000 series, with white lettering on the 2030 and gold-plated lettering on the 2050. New control knobs featuring numbered edges were standard, but some Hamburgs and El Dorados have been seen with the silver-top knobs as used on the 4000-series basses. The 2030 and 2050 were superseded by the 2020 and 2060 in 1992.

The 2050 El Dorado gets the deluxe treatment with a double-bound body and gold-plated hardware. Numbered knobs were standard on both the 2030 and 2050, but standard Rickenbacker knobs appear on many. Gold-plated Rickenbacker-labled Schaller tuners were exclusive to the El Dorado. Larry Bolt photos.

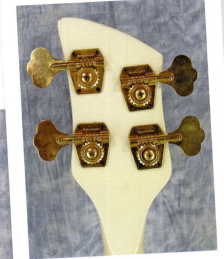

(Below) Height-adjustable spring-loaded fittings were glued to the bottom of each pickup. Allen bolts in the back of the body screwed into the fittings. Chris Dombrowski photo.

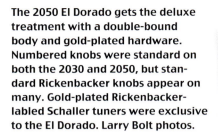

(Left and below) The control pots, microswitch, and output jack were attached to the printed circuit board. Note the recess cut in the edge of the body for the output. Jeff Rath photos.

2030 Hamburg Identifying Features

Blade-shaped headstock was similar to that on the 3001. Blackened tuners accompanied finishes such as Mapleglo (here), White, Silver, and Red.

The neck-body mounting plate carries the engraved serial number. The Allen bolts in the back adjust pickup height. Large black plate covers the control cavity. Note the recess for the output jack.

The "bolt-on" necks of both the 2030 and 2050 were bound, usually with white plastic, but this Mapleglo example has black binding. Only the 2050 El Dorado had body binding. Jeff Rath photos.

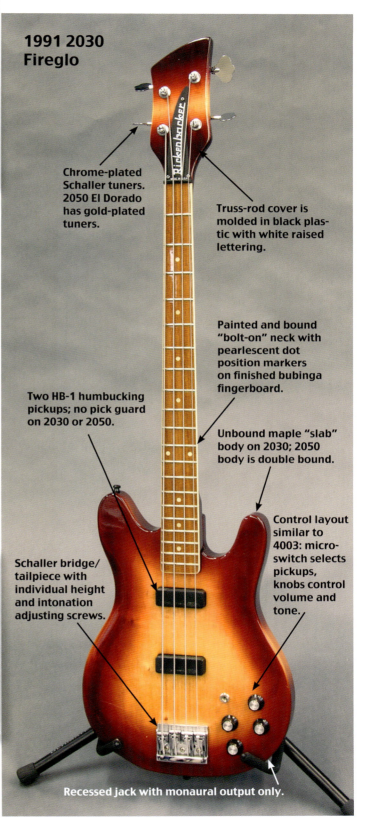

1991 2030 Fireglo

Chrome-plated Schaller tuners. 2050 El Dorado has gold-plated tuners.

Truss-rod cover is molded in black plastic with white raised lettering.

Painted and bound "bolt-on" neck with pearlescent dot position markers on finished bubinga fingerboard.

Two HB-1 humbucking pickups; no pick guard on 2030 or 2050.

Unbound maple "slab" body on 2030; 2050 body is double bound.

Control layout similar to 4003: micro-switch selects pickups, knobs control volume and tone.

Schaller bridge/tailpiece with individual height and intonation adjusting screws.

Recessed jack with monaural output only.

4001V63

A salute to the '60s

1984 – 2002

Shortly after the cancellation of the 4003SB, a new vintage series was introduced in late 1984. The "V" series resulted in much more accurate replicas of the iconic instruments that powered the music of the mid-1960s, and in particular, those played by many of the stars of the British Invasion. The bass in this line, the 4001V63, captured nearly every physical detail of the 4001S and Rose Morris 1999 of that era.

Old is new again

Though labeled "4001," the new bass was structurally similar to the 4003S with its better truss-rod system and improved electronics. RIC produced new "vintage" pickups for this bass, redesigned versions of the iconic Toaster-top and Horseshoe. Some early production V63 basses had genuine old-style Horseshoe pickups, identified by four screw poles on the top of the bobbin, covered by magnetized steel horseshoes. Most V63 basses had a new "reissue" Horseshoe. This was actually a modified High-gain pickup with Alnico magnetic poles within the body of the pickup, rather than the horseshoe magnets of the original. The new pickup's "shoes" are not magnetized but provide shielding. They can be removed at the minor cost of increased hum and decreased output. A new pickup surround with a flared bottom was also developed to look like the historic version.

Completing the scene was a retro tailpiece with its characteristic gap in the center tooth of the mute cover. One concession was the five-screw mount: The original tailpiece was anchored by only three. Old-style black control knobs were provided, and the back heel of the neck was squared off as it flared to the body. The headstock was elongated and carried walnut "head wings." It also featured the old-style clear acrylic truss-rod cover with lettering and background painted on the back.

Production refinements on the V63 paralleled changes in other Rickenbacker basses of the time. The shape of the headstocks were standardized in the mid-1990s, resulting in a chunkier look with a shorter "throat" above the nut. This is easily seen on newer V63s as it places the acrylic truss-rod cover higher on the headstock, with its point nearly reaching the top of the head.

Colors

According to the company literature the 4001V63 was available in Fireglo and Mapleglo only, but Jetglo examples are not uncommon. Occasionally, the factory will set aside perfectly good instruments that have unattractive charac-

A little bit of flame licks the side of this 1999 Mapleglo 4001V63.

4001V63 Identifying Features

(Left) Early V63s featured a headstock with a longer "throat." (Right) Starting in the mid-1990s, the headstock shape had a shorter "throat."

Vintage models feature a squared-off neck heel.

The reissued Toaster-top pickup is placed a half inch from the fingerboard. The V63's pick guard extends nearly to the frame of the reissued Horseshoe pickup.

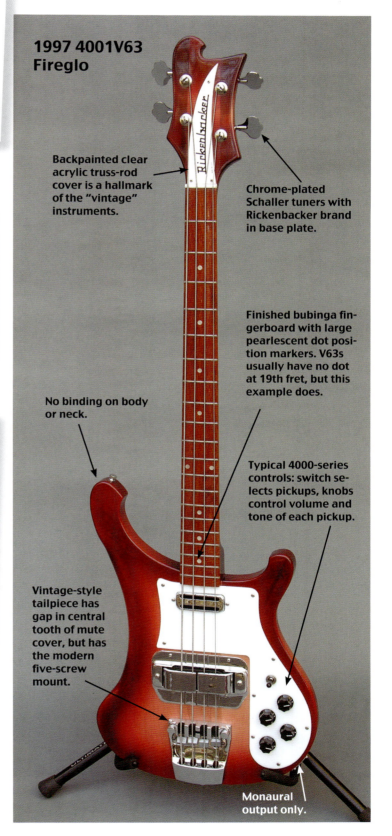

1997 4001V63 Fireglo

Backpainted clear acrylic truss-rod cover is a hallmark of the "vintage" instruments.

Chrome-plated Schaller tuners with Rickenbacker brand in base plate.

Finished bubinga fingerboard with large pearlescent dot position markers. V63s usually have no dot at 19th fret, but this example does.

No binding on body or neck.

Typical 4000-series controls: switch selects pickups, knobs control volume and tone of each pickup.

Vintage-style tailpiece has gap in central tooth of mute cover, but has the modern five-screw mount.

Monaural output only.

Unusual colors for V63s: (Below) A 2002 finished in metallic Midnight Blue. Chris Harris photo. (Near right) Several V63s got the handsome Jetglo finish like this 1999 example. (Far right) The stunning Sea Green adorns this V63 made in 2000; probably only a half dozen received this color. Steve Wood photo.

One of only a handful of 4001V63 basses finished in metallic Turquoise. (Below) A pair of rare lefty 4001V63 basses. The Mapleglo has the standard headstock. Mandy L. Montanye/Music Go Round photo. The Fireglo example features the "PMC" optional flipped headstock.

teristics in the wood for the application of an opaque finish.

As production extended into the 2000s, the factory applied other colors to a few V63s. Just a handful were finished in Midnight Blue (a deep metallic blue), Turquoise (metallic blue-green), and Sea Green (a brilliant aquamarine). Sea Green was the first of RIC's new "Color of the Year" program started in 2000.

PMC option

Though not widely advertised, left-handed versions of the 4001V63 were available with an optional "PMC" head-stock. The lettering was an abbreviation for Paul McCartney, and the option allowed for a flip of the headstock shape to resemble Sir Paul's famous Fireglo 4001S from 1964. Back then (and until the 1980s), left-handed basses had the same neck/headstock planks as right-handed instruments (so they looked "upside down") and had special printed truss-rod covers applied so the Rickenbacker name wouldn't read upside down.

The PMC option was applied to many instruments made in 1999 and exported to Japan, where enthusiastic players and collectors appreciate the replication of every minor detail. The new 4001C64 and C64S vintage models that followed the V63 series in 2002 embraced the design cue of the PMC option, even allowing for upside-down headstocks for right-handers!

The last V63 was produced in 2002.

4003S/5

Get down deeper

1986 – 2002

Disco was dying. Rap was on the rise. Compact discs were developed and vinyl vanished. It was the 1980s, and music was changing; you can decide for yourself if it was for the better or the worse. But everyone wanted more BASS! And the lower the frequency, the better! Sub-woofers started filling up trunk space in cars and gave new meaning to "rumbling down the road."

So, how do you create lower frequencies? Digital sound generation was one answer. Synthesizers and digital key-boards could easily plumb the depths. But what could be done with the traditional bass guitar? Just tuning down the low E string on a bass was impractical past a full step or two. So, what was needed was a heavier string that could provide low frequency at playable tension. Five-string basses began to appear with a low B string added to the normal E, A, D, and G.

First five

Rickenbacker answered the demand in 1986 with its first five-string bass, the 4003S/5, a slight redesign of the down-trimmed 4003S. The headstock was reshaped with the left side (as viewed from the front) extended closer to the nut to accommodate a fifth tuner. The tuners were chrome-plated (or black chrome) Schaller M4 units. The nut was cut with five grooves, and two new pieces of hardware were developed: A High-gain pickup with a five-pole bobbin was installed in the treble position, along with a bridge assembly that held five saddles in place of the usual four. The classic tailpiece, with its under-string mute, was modified with the removal of the "teeth" over the mute, and the middle two apertures at the bottom were made into one large opening to route the E, A, and D strings to their anchors. The tailpiece was usually

This five-string bass, made in 1982, can be considered an experimental prototype. It's clearly made on a 4008 chassis with a custom made five-pole treble pickup, a rudimentary drop-in bridge, and modified tailpiece. Ron O'Keefe photos.

A fine 2001 example of the five-banger 4003S/5 in Midnight Blue. The treble pickup cover has been removed to reveal the specially made five-pole High-gain bobbin. Bill Henshell photo.

drilled out for seven mounting screws, but some have five, missing the pair of screws at the bottom. Rickenbacker's classic Toaster-top pickup was used in the bass (neck) position. Only the standard monaural output was fitted. A few LH (left-handed) fivers were produced. The dimensions of the neck were roughly the same as those of a standard four-string Rickenbacker.

Developmental prototype

At least one experimental five-string bass was made before the final design reached production. A Jetglo example made in May 1982 was lashed up on a 4008 chassis with its bound neck, long headstock, and modified tailpiece. It featured five streamlined Schaller tuners and a five-pole treble pickup. The bridge was a custom-built, five-saddle unit resembling the ones installed on the 4005 hollow-body basses but made to fit the pocket in the classic tailpiece. This predates the final five-saddle bridge fitted to the production models.

The 4003S/5 formed the basis for the rare all-black 4003SPC/5 five-string Blackstar in the last couple of years of the '80s (p. 92). By 2002, the 4003S/5 was gone from the price sheets, replaced by the short-lived 4004Cii/5 Cheyenne II.

(Left) A 1997 4003S/5 in metallic Turquoise. Ron O'Keefe photo. (Below) One of the last 4003S/5s made, this 2002 instrument is finished in Maplglo.

4003S/5 Identifying Features

The headstock of the 4003S/5 has a longer "wing" on the B, E, A side to accommodate the extra Schaller M4 tuner. Ron O'Keefe photo.

A new five-pole High-gain pickup was developed for this model.

The tailpiece had the "teeth" of the mute cover removed and an enlarged hole in the center to route three strings. A new five-saddle bridge was made to fit in the standard pocket.

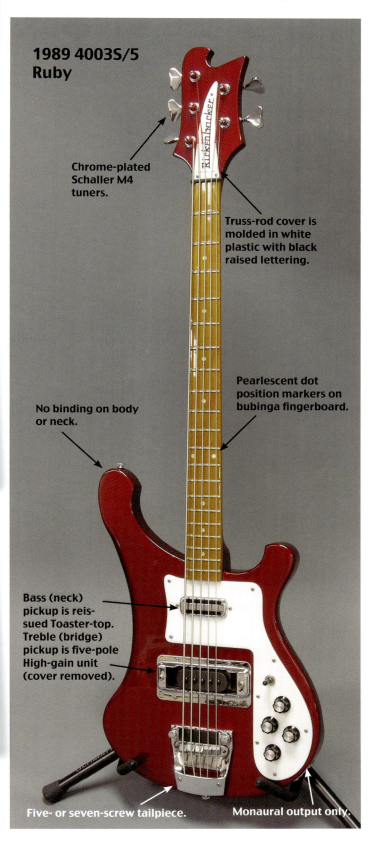

1989 4003S/5 Ruby

Chrome-plated Schaller M4 tuners.

Truss-rod cover is molded in white plastic with black raised lettering.

Pearlescent dot position markers on bubinga fingerboard.

No binding on body or neck.

Bass (neck) pickup is reissued Toaster-top. Treble (bridge) pickup is five-pole High-gain unit (cover removed).

Five- or seven-screw tailpiece.

Monaural output only.

4003S/8

Last of the eight-bangers

1986 – 2002

At first glance, the 4003S/8 looks the same as the 4008. Get a few steps closer, though, and the differences become apparent. The headstock is a bit larger, with more curves compared with the old 4008 head. However the modern chrome-plated Schaller M4 tuners were retained. Like its stablemates 4003S and 4003S/5, the 4003S/8 has no binding on the body or neck. Dot position markers are present once again, and the body is the typical unbound example of the classic Rick bass.

The tailpiece was less dramatically modified than the unit installed on the old 4008. Since the strings were closely paired, it was unnecessary to eliminate the "teeth" over the mute. Likewise, the string routes at the butt end of the tailpiece could also accommodate the strings without interference. So, they were left intact. Underneath, eight holes were drilled in the bottom of the casting for the ball ends of the strings. Seven wood screws fasten the tailpiece sturdily to the body.

Once again, each pair of strings shared one saddle. Unlike the previous 4008, the 4003S/8 had the lighter octave string to the right of the standard bass string (viewing the upright instrument), favoring those who pluck with the fingertips. Pick players who prefer the alternative setup often replace the nut and re-groove the saddles so the octave string is to the left. This assures the player that the downward stroke of the pick gets a good bite on the brighter-sounding string.

The classic six-pole Toaster-top pickup is set an inch from the fingerboard, while a standard four-pole High-gain pickup sits in the cavity near the tailpiece. As with the 4003S and 4003S/5, only the standard monaural output is installed.

First appearing in 1986, the 4003S/8 stayed in production until sometime in 2002.

This 1994 Mapleglo 4003S/8 has a High-gain pickup in the bass (neck) position, although the Toaster-top pickup was the norm.

4003S/8 Identifying Features

The headstock of the 4003S/8 was a bit larger than that of the old 4008. This Jetglo example from 1998 has black trim including the truss-rod cover.

The reissued Toaster-top pickup was standard in the bass (neck) position.

Unlike that on the old 4008, the tailpiece of the 4003S/8 retained the "teeth" on the mute cover and four separate routing holes for the strings.

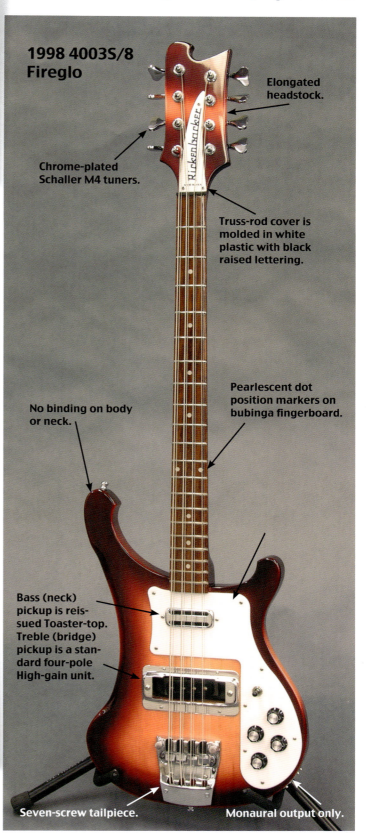

1998 4003S/8 Fireglo

Elongated headstock.

Chrome-plated Schaller M4 tuners.

Truss-rod cover is molded in white plastic with black raised lettering.

Pearlescent dot position markers on bubinga fingerboard.

No binding on body or neck.

Bass (neck) pickup is reissued Toaster-top. Treble (bridge) pickup is a standard four-pole High-gain unit.

Seven-screw tailpiece.

Monaural output only.

4003SPC Specials

Blackstar, Redneck, and Tuxedo 1987 – 1990

(Left) Near mint examples of all three SPC models pose for the author's camera. Note the once-White Tuxedo has aged to a cream color. (Above) RIC's publicity photo features Tom Petty (right) and Mike Campbell showing off brand new 4003SPC Redneck basses, including a rare eight-string model, much like this one (right).

In the late 1980s, Rickenbacker produced three certified limited-run basses designated "4003SPC" and dubbed "Blackstar," "Redneck," and "Tuxedo." Based on the 4003S model with no binding and monaural-only output, they were made with maple fingerboards instead of the usual bubinga. Tiny "pin-dot" position markers, instead of the usual larger pearlescent dots, were applied to the faces of the boards. The big difference was the monochromatic paint schemes covering even the fingerboards. Each of the specials had black trim, including black truss-rod covers with raised white lettering, black plastic pick guards, and blackened hardware. The Blackstar differed slightly with chromed bass-pickup surround, treble-pickup cover, mute adjustment screws, strap pins, and truss-rod-cover lettering.

Production of the SPC models began in early 1987 with the Tuxedo. The Redneck and Blackstar appeared in late 1987. The Redneck was produced into early 1988, and the Blackstar was continued into early 1990. According to

(Above) Mike Mesaros, one-time bassist of the Smithereens, poses with a Blackstar in this RIC publicity photo. (Left) Blackstars are rare enough, but only a handful of five-string Blackstars were made.

the certificates that accompanied each instrument, 200 Blackstars, 125 Rednecks, and 100 or 125 Tuxedos were issued. The initial Tuxedo run was 100, but evidence suggests runs of 15 and 10 were added later to fulfill demand. Even so, it is not clear whether the entire intended production run of each model was completed.

The Blackstar was the only one of the three SPCs to be featured on RIC price lists. The June 1989 retail price list states that both four- and five-string Blackstars ($1,169 and $1,369 respectively) were available. Several eight-string Rednecks were made, and at least one left-handed Tuxedo has been documented. The Tuxedo was the only one of the three schemes to be applied to Rickenbacker guitars; the six- and twelve-string 360/370 Tuxedos.

4003SPC Identifying Features

The maple fingerboard is painted along with the rest of the bass: Red on Redneck; Jetglo on Blackstar; White on Tuxedo. Tiny "pin dot" position markers are used on all SPC basses. White often turns a cream color.

"Blackstar" has chromed pickup covers and mute adjustment screws. Some SPCs came with vintage knobs, some with standard knobs.

1988 4003SPC Redneck

Black Schaller tuners.

Truss-rod cover is molded in black plastic with raised lettering painted white.

No binding on body or neck.

Rickenbacker's "Red" is brilliant, solid, fire-engine red, not metallic.

Black plastic pick guard.

Both pickups are High-gain units with blackened covers. The plastic treble (bridge) pickup cover has been removed from this example.

Five- or seven-screw tailpiece.

Monaural output only.

4001CS

Chris Squire Limited Edition 1990 – 2000

Chris Squire poses in the California twilight for this RIC advertising portrait accompanying the launch of the CS series. (Left) A beautifully restored 1991 4001CS from the author's collection.

The one musician most recognizable with a Rickenbacker bass in hand is surely Chris Squire of Yes. Originally a Fireglo RM 1999, Chris's Rick has been repaired, refinished, and modified several times since he purchased it in 1964. Its familiar cream color and exposed headstock wings set the color palette for Rickenbacker's first "signature" limited-edition bass.

A spinoff of the 4001V63, the 4001CS has the same hardware and overall features but is equipped with deluxe vermillion wood fingerboard and headstock wings. The pick guard is clear acrylic, backpainted with a printed Chris Squire signature in black on a white background. The cream paint replicates Squire's classic Rick but often yellows more with age and exposure to the elements.

Production of the Chris Squire bass was limited to 1,000, and each was accompanied by a certificate stating the instrument's sequence number within the production run. The first CS bass was issued in mid-1990, and the last rolled off the line in early 2000.

Like the similar 4001V63, the CS experienced production tweaks along the way, including the shape of the headstock and bridge-pickup surround.

4001CS Identifying Features

The pickguard is clear acrylic and backpainted with Chris Squire's signature and a white background.

Only a handful of lefty 4001CS basses are to be found in the wild. This one was captured by Ronn Roberts and shot by Steven Mackie Photography.

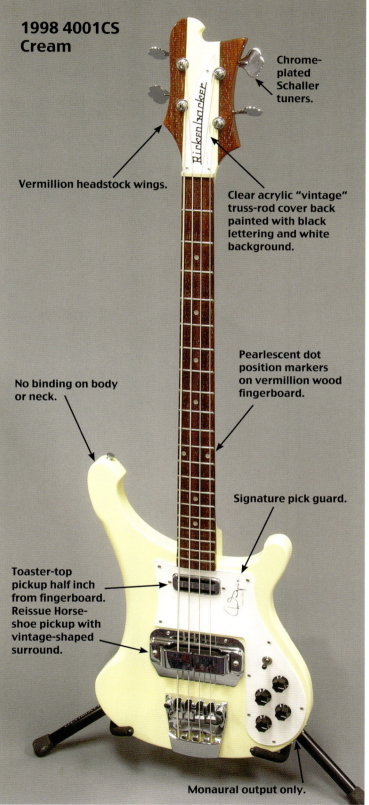

1998 4001CS Cream

Chrome-plated Schaller tuners.

Vermillion headstock wings.

Clear acrylic "vintage" truss-rod cover back painted with black lettering and white background.

No binding on body or neck.

Pearlescent dot position markers on vermillion wood fingerboard.

Signature pick guard.

Toaster-top pickup half inch from fingerboard. Reissue Horseshoe pickup with vintage-shaped surround.

Monaural output only.

2020, 2060, and 2030GF

Rickenbacker's next-gen Hamburg, the El Dorado, and the Glenn Frey signature edition

1992 – 1995

The ultimate development of the Hamburg and El Dorado basses came about in 1992. The big change from the 2030/2050 was in the electronics. HB-2 humbucking pickups were retained, but the new models featured a new control layout, similar to the setup on the new 4004-series basses introduced the same year. Gone was the printed circuit board with its characteristic recessed jack. In its place was a simplified arrangement of a three-way microswitch to select the pickups (bass/both/treble) and single volume and tone pots. These were all mounted on a small pointed-teardrop pick guard and rested in a cavity cut in the top of the body. The jack was mounted on a plate along the lower edge of the body.

You look different

Like the earlier models, the Hamburg's body was unbound; the El Dorado's body was double-bound, usually with white plastic. Unlike their predecessors, the necks of both models were unpainted and unbound. Another difference was the change from bubinga to maple fingerboard with small black position markers, similar to the boards on the new 4004 series.

Hardware changes included modern Schaller M4 tuners and an ABM bridge. The neck was attached to the body with wood screws through a backing plate that carried the engraved serial number. Once again, Allen-head bolts in the back of the body controlled the height of the pickups.

Most 2020 Hamburg basses had chrome-plated hardware, but a few finish colors called for black trim: In those cases, blackened bridge, tuners, and strap pins accompanied a black plastic pick guard. El Dorado basses featured gold-plated hardware, and some color schemes may have been fitted with black pick guard and binding. All basses of this design had metal knobs and jackplates plated in either chrome or gold.

A subtle change on the unbound 2020 was the contouring of both edges of the body top; only the top front edge of the older 2030 and 3001 was contoured.

Looking great in Turquoise, the top-of-the-line 2060 El Dorado shows off its maple fingerboard, gold-plated hardware, and double-bound body. Steve Wood photo.

2060 El Dorado Identifying Features

The maple neck, fingerboard, and blade-shaped headstock are unpainted. The face of the headstock is clear coated.

The neck/body mounting plate carries the engraved serial number. The Allen bolts in the back adjust the pickup height.

Controls and wiring were similar to the 4004 series basses, but mounted to a tear-drop shaped plastic pick guard. Microswitch selects pickups, knobs control overall volume and overall tone.

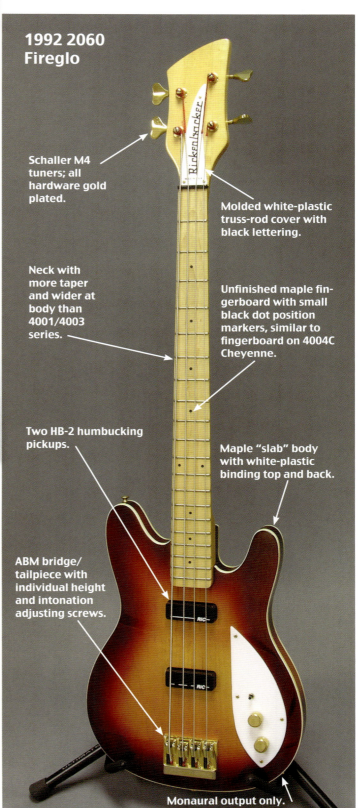

1992 2060 Fireglo

Schaller M4 tuners; all hardware gold plated.

Molded white-plastic truss-rod cover with black lettering.

Neck with more taper and wider at body than 4001/4003 series.

Unfinished maple fingerboard with small black dot position markers, similar to fingerboard on 4004C Cheyenne.

Two HB-2 humbucking pickups.

Maple "slab" body with white-plastic binding top and back.

ABM bridge/tailpiece with individual height and intonation adjusting screws.

Monaural output only.

Glenn Frey signature edition

The first of the new models to appear was the 2030GF Glenn Frey signature edition. While structurally and electronically identical to the new 2020 bass, the Glenn Frey instrument retained the old designation (along with its partnered 230GF guitar). Apparently, the 2020 and 2060 model numbers were chosen *after* the 2030 Glenn Frey instruments appeared on the March 1992 price list.

The 2030GF basses came with a certificate stating the production number within a run of 1,000, but it is thought that both guitars and basses were included in this production total; likely, fewer than 100 2030GF basses were made.

All Glenn Frey instruments featured a Jetglo finish overall – even the fingerboard with its pin-dot position markers, à la the 4003SPC Blackstar. Blackened tuners, bridge, and strap pins were installed. The pick guard was clear acrylic with the black-printed Glenn Frey signature and a silver paint background. The truss-rod cover was also clear acrylic with back-painted black lettering and silver background.

Although the 230GF guitar was included through the January 2000 price list, the 2030GF, 2020 Hamburg, and 2060 El Dorado basses disappeared from the December 1995 and subsequent listings.

(Left) A Turquoise 2020 Hamburg showing the unbound body, contoured edges of the top, and chrome-plated hardware. John Minutaglio photo. (Above) A page from the 1995 RIC catalog shows a Fireglo 2020 Hamburg and a Mapleglo 2060 El Dorado (misspelled as one word) along with the accompanying guitars. (Right) A promotion sheet for the Glenn Frey signature edition instruments misses an "n" from the name – right under the signature! Note the missing "0" from the model number, too. It should read "2030GF."

2030 Glenn Frey Identifying Features

Blade-shaped headstock of the 2000 series basses is similar, but not identical to, the 3000 series heads. Truss-rod cover is clear acrylic, back-painted with black lettering and silver background – unique to the Glenn Frey Signature Edition. Jeff Thomas photos.

Following its nearly all-black color scheme, the ABM bridge is black, and the RIC legends on the faces of the HB-2 pickups have been blacked out.

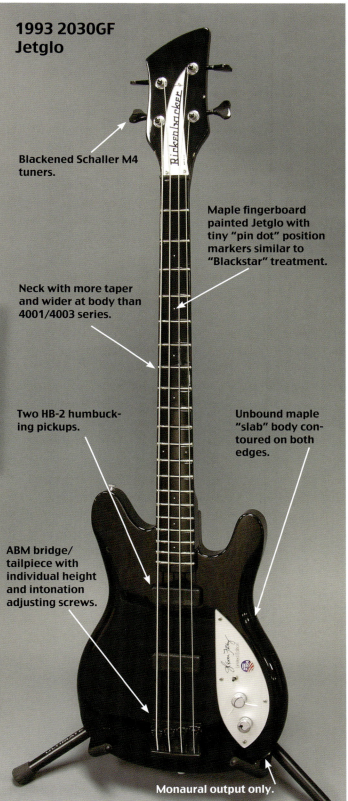

1993 2030GF Jetglo

Blackened Schaller M4 tuners.

Neck with more taper and wider at body than 4001/4003 series.

Two HB-2 humbucking pickups.

ABM bridge/ tailpiece with individual height and intonation adjusting screws.

Maple fingerboard painted Jetglo with tiny "pin dot" position markers similar to "Blackstar" treatment.

Unbound maple "slab" body contoured on both edges.

Monaural output only.

Tear-drop shaped pick guard is also clear acrylic, back-painted with Glenn Frey's signature and silver background. Control knobs on all 2000-series basses are chrome- or gold-plated metal.

4004C Cheyenne
Streamlining the classic Rick bass
1992 – 1999

As the advertisement (right) states, "The *revolution* continues." In 1992, Rickenbacker developed a brand-new line of basses that retained the classic shape of the solid-body 4000-series instrument, but with a modern take. The ad goes on to say, "The Cheyenne evolved from one of the most popular, most recognized basses in history. It redefines industry standards. Our new bridge design allows for easier adjustment, while our high-output humbucking pickups produce even more of that distinctive Rickenbacker sound. For a smoother, faster feel, we hand-craft the neck from Eastern Maple running the full length of the bass. The body is sculpted from American grown solid Walnut. Also available all black as the 4004L Laredo. Feel the revolution."

So, what's new?

The new design still featured a neck-through-body construction, but with a slightly tapered neck that was wider at the body than the 4001/4003 series basses. Instead of the trusty single-coil pickups, Rickenbacker went with the HB-1 humbuckers with the same footprint as the old Toaster-top and High-gain units. Both pickups are mounted with wood screws to shallow depressions on the top surface. Foam material under the mounting ring allows some degree of adjustment of pickup height.

The controls were also simplified, with a small three-way switch to select the pickups (bass/both/treble), and single volume and tone knobs. The pots and wire harness were loaded into a pocket cut from the rear of the body

and covered with a plastic cap. The bridge was an ABM unit with individual roller-saddle height adjusted by small Allen screws, and intonation by Phillips machine screws from the rear of the bridge body. Standard production Cheyennes and Laredos had no pick guards, mutes, or Rick-O-Sound outputs.

Tuning keys were streamlined Schaller M4 units. Hardware was gold-plated on the Cheyenne, and chrome-plated on the Laredo. The truss-rod covers were molded in black plastic with gold letters on the 4004C and chrome letters on the 4004L.

Introduction

The 4004C Cheyenne and 4004L Laredo debuted in late 1992, and the first Cheyenne, a lefty, was given to Paul McCartney. From debut until 1999, the Cheyenne featured a maple neck-through-body plank, maple fingerboard, and figured walnut body and head wings. The Cheyenne (or Cheyenne I, as it came to be known) could be maintained with "oil finish." The contouring of the 4004 design and the walnut body wings made the 4004C the lightest Rickenbacker bass ever, coming in at around nine pounds.

A prime example of the classy 4004C Cheyenne from 1993. This bass from the author's collection has been modified by having the microswitch replaced by a second volume pot, resulting in separate volume controls for each pickup. The third knob controls tone.

RCA specials

Some of the first Cheyenne basses were made for RCA Records Nashville, which ordered guitars and basses to give to its best-selling artists. Little is known of these instruments, and it is likely only three or four RCA basses were made. They were like the walnut-body Cheyenne but had chrome (instead of gold) hardware, a gold back-painted acrylic truss-rod cover with black lettering, and a special gold-back-painted acrylic pick guard that featured the RCA logo and "Nipper" the dog listening to "his master's voice" from a gramophone.

Along with the RCA guitar and bass order, Rickenbacker made a special lefty double-neck instrument for an RCA's executive at the time. It was a lashup of the Cheyenne bass and a 650S Sierra six-string guitar with gold hardware and no pick guard. The truss-rod cover on the bass neck held the Rickenbacker label, the one on the guitar neck had the dog and gramophone. This snapshot of it resting on a rack at the factory (above) is the only known photo of this unique instrument.

(Left) The ultra-rare RCA Special was based on the new 4004C Cheyenne. John Minutaglio photo.

4004C Identifying Features

Angled neck "heel" is a hallmark of the 4004 family.

Wiring and controls are inside a cavity in the back of the body and protected by a black-plastic cover.

ABM bridge/tailpiece has individual height and intonation adjusting screws.

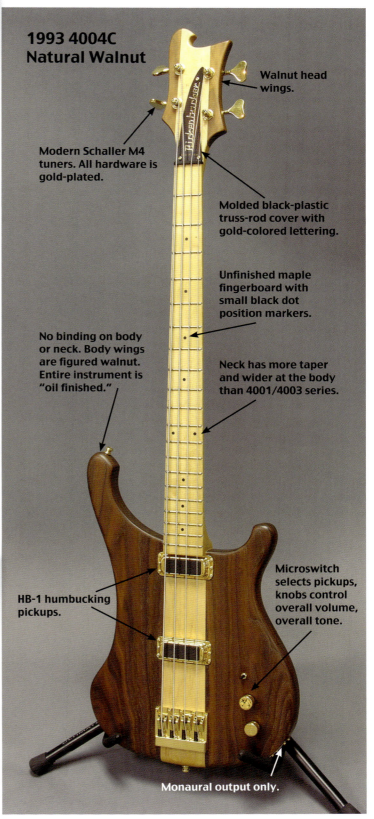

**1993 4004C
Natural Walnut**

Walnut head wings.

Modern Schaller M4 tuners. All hardware is gold-plated.

Molded black-plastic truss-rod cover with gold-colored lettering.

Unfinished maple fingerboard with small black dot position markers.

No binding on body or neck. Body wings are figured walnut. Entire instrument is "oil finished."

Neck has more taper and wider at the body than 4001/4003 series.

HB-1 humbucking pickups.

Microswitch selects pickups, knobs control overall volume, overall tone.

Monaural output only.

4004L Laredo

Clean and powerful

1992 –

Developed in parallel with the 4004C Cheyenne, the 4004L Laredo first appeared in late 1992 in one guise: Jetglo with a clear finished maple fingerboard and chrome hardware, matching Rickenbacker's 650C Colorado guitar. The Laredo's introductory Jetglo finish also gave the factory some flexibility, allowing the body wings to be made of maple, walnut, or other hardwoods, then simply covered in black paint. However, most were made of solid maple. The Laredo's maple fingerboard often featured birdseye figuring.

All the electronics and hardware were the same as that fitted to the Cheyenne, only chrome- instead of gold-plated. A black-plastic molded truss-rod cover with chrome-plated raised lettering was standard on the Laredos. After the first couple of years of production, Rickenbacker did away with the Jetglo-only description in its literature, and alternate finishes began appearing on the Laredo.

Relocated pickups

Some of the feature changes made to the Cheyenne II (see p. 108) around 1999 were brought over to the Laredo. The first change was lowering both pickups toward the bridge. The change from maple to bubinga fingerboard with small pearlescent dot position markers followed shortly thereafter. By 2000, these features were standard.

Laredo bodies were usually built with maple wings, but, on rare occasions, Laredos from 2000 onward were constructed with maple/walnut/maple body wings normally destined for the 4004Cii Cheyenne II. These would usually be finished in an opaque color that would conceal the construction, but a peek inside the control cavity would reveal the body-wing assembly. Early maple and later bubinga fingerboards were usually clear-coated on Laredos.

As with the Cheyenne II, the pickups were repositioned to the original design locations by 2005 to ease replacement of truss rods when necessary. Also like the Cheyenne II, a Schaller bridge replaced the ABM unit on Laredos in 2007. In 2011, RIC reshaped the neck profile to match that of the flagship 4003; in other words, the fingerboard was narrower where it met the body. The wood used for the fingerboard was switched from bubinga to chechen in 2011.

A 1993 4004L Laredo dressed in the premiere finish of Jetglo and natural maple fingerboard. Mike Parks/The Music Connection photo.

4004L Identifying Features

All hardware on the 4004L Laredo is chrome-plated. Tuners are Schaller M4 units.

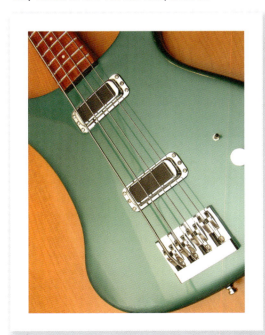

Wiring and controls are tucked into a cavity in the back of the body. Note the body wing construction of this Turquoise Laredo is maple/walnut/maple, usually found in the 4004Cii Cheyenne II.

From late 1999 to 2004, pickups on the Laredo and Cheyenne II were mounted closer to the bridge.

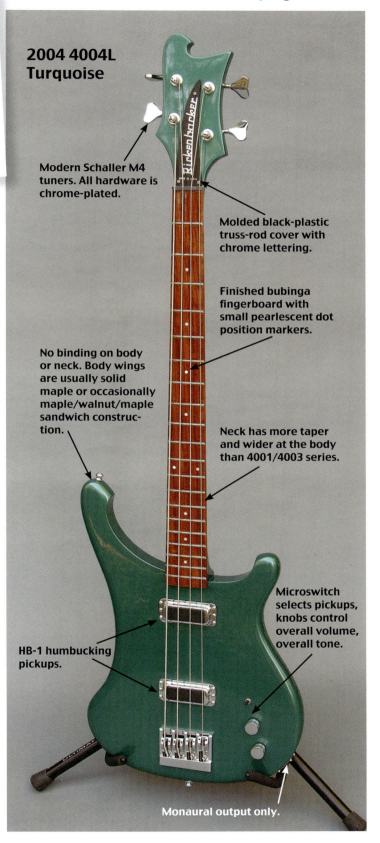

2004 4004L Turquoise

Modern Schaller M4 tuners. All hardware is chrome-plated.

Molded black-plastic truss-rod cover with chrome lettering.

Finished bubinga fingerboard with small pearlescent dot position markers.

No binding on body or neck. Body wings are usually solid maple or occasionally maple/walnut/maple sandwich construction.

Neck has more taper and wider at the body than 4001/4003 series.

Microswitch selects pickups, knobs control overall volume, overall tone.

HB-1 humbucking pickups.

Monaural output only.

(Above) A 2012 4004L in Ruby. Starting in late 2011, Rickenbacker has made fingerboards from chechen instead of bubinga. Jeff Scott photo.

(Far left) This Red 4004L was fitted with "piccolo" strings – the high-octave strings from a set for an eight-string bass.

(Middle left) A 1997 4004L in Fireglo from the author's collection. It has the volume/volume/tone control modification and a swapped-out white truss-rod cover.

(Near left) A 2001 Laredo in the "Color of the Year," Desert Gold. RIC used bubinga fingerboards on 4004 basses from 1999 – 2011. Mike Parks / The Music Connection photo.

(Right) Another 1999 Laredo in Midnight Blue shows transitional features of that year. Pickups have been "lowered," but it still has the maple fingerboard. The pick guard is a custom addition.

4004Cii Cheyenne II

Not just a pretty face
1999 –

Fire and flame: A gorgeously flamed 2008 4004Cii in the 2006 Color of the Year, Amber Fireglo. Photo by Wildwood Guitars.

In 1999, Rickenbacker introduced an improved version of the 4004C Cheyenne. The new model was officially designated 4004Cii (the "ii" meaning "bis," French for "second"), but most call it the Cheyenne II.

It appears that the new model stemmed from experiments with an increased supply of attractively figured maple and reduced supply of premium walnut. A prototype that is stored in the company museum in Santa Ana, California, has a beautiful quilted maple top (front) laminated to the typical Cheyenne assembly of walnut body wings and a maple neck-through plank. This particular instrument carries a maple fingerboard and an overall clear satin finish.

Early production
Rickenbacker started to modify the Cheyenne design (as well as that of the 4004L Laredo), first with a move of both pickups an inch toward the bridge to take advantage of tonal nodes. A little later, RIC substituted bubinga fingerboards in place of the maple ones, and they featured small pearlescent dot position markers rather than black ones.

It seems the first batch of Cheyenne IIs took advantage of more quilted maple like that used on the museum example. A few Maplegло basses with quilted tops, walnut backs, lowered pickups, and bubinga fingerboards were issued, including a beautiful lefty shown here. Not many Cheyenne IIs were made with this body style, because good walnut was getting more difficult to obtain. A change to body wings made from a maple/walnut/maple sandwich construction quickly followed. This remains the standard for Cheyenne IIs. Most 4004Cii's have figured maple tops and backs, but not many are blessed with the stunning quilt patterns of the early examples. "Flamed"

or "tiger-striped" maple on Cheyenne IIs is typical.

Cheyenne II bodies are contoured around most of the edges, except where the jackplate is mounted. The bevel at the butt end of the upper wing is not as pronounced as it was on the original Cheyenne. Around the time of the appearance of the sandwiched bodies, maple wings on the headstocks were introduced. Walnut head wings returned around 2006.

(Above left) This developmental prototype of the Cheyenne II resides at the Rickenbacker company museum. It features a quilted maple top, walnut back (above center), the original-style maple fingerboard, and a clear satin finish. RIC photos by Richard Cannata. (Above right) A rare, lefty, early production Cii shows a bubinga fingerboard, lowered pickups to go along with the quilted maple top, and walnut back. Photo by Dave Fisher.

(Above) Andy Lewis performs with Paul Weller playing a 2004 Cheyenne II in Montezuma Brown. Stefan Durr photo. (Right) A stunning 2000 quilted-maple lefty Cii in Trans Red.

Like the earlier 4004C, hardware is gold-plated and the truss-rod cover is molded black plastic with gold-plated lettering.

There and back again

The position of the pickups was returned to the original locations on Cheyenne IIs (and Laredos) by 2005 when it was determined that in the rare case of a truss-rod failure, it was difficult to remove a rod without having a pickup route in the body at the end of the fingerboard.

Most bubinga fingerboards on Cheyenne IIs are "unfinished" (likely having only a sealer coat), but some examples have clear-gloss-coated boards. A hardware change to the Cheyenne II (and Laredo) was made in 2007 when the ABM bridge was replaced with a Schaller unit like the ones used on the earlier 2030/2050 basses. Late in 2010, the neck-through body plank became a two-piece structure with a narrower taper similar to the 4003 flagship. Also, the wood used on the fingerboards was switched to chechen in late 2011.

4004Cii Cheyenne II Identifying Features

Current production 4004Cii headstocks feature contrasting walnut "wings."

All but the first batch of 4004Cii basses feature body wings with maple/walnut/maple sandwich construction.

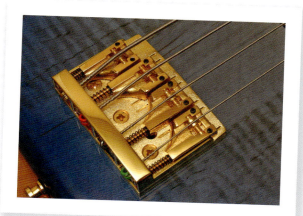

The current-production 4004Cii features a Schaller bridge/tailpiece with individual height and intonation adjusting screws.

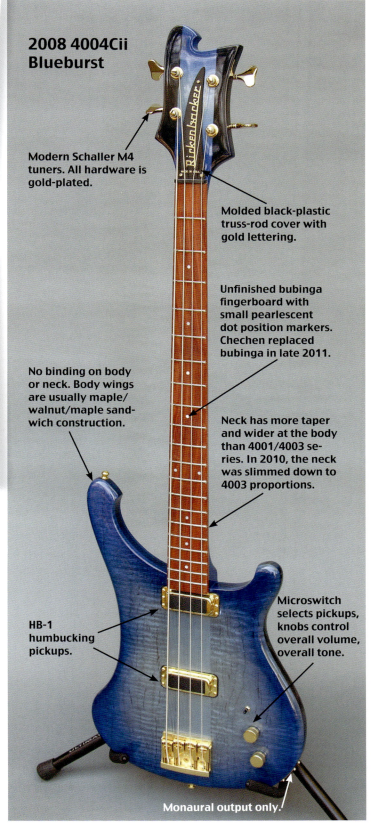

2008 4004Cii Blueburst

Modern Schaller M4 tuners. All hardware is gold-plated.

Molded black-plastic truss-rod cover with gold lettering.

Unfinished bubinga fingerboard with small pearlescent dot position markers. Chechen replaced bubinga in late 2011.

No binding on body or neck. Body wings are usually maple/walnut/maple sandwich construction.

Neck has more taper and wider at the body than 4001/4003 series. In 2010, the neck was slimmed down to 4003 proportions.

HB-1 humbucking pickups.

Microswitch selects pickups, knobs control overall volume, overall tone.

Monaural output only.

(Left to right) A 2003 Cii in Mapleglo with maple head wings. A rare 2004 Cii in that year's "Color of the Year," Blue Boy. A handsome 2004 Cii in Jetglo. A 2004 five-banger Cii/5 in Mapleglo. All these Cheyenne IIs have their pickups in the "lowered" positions.

Special colors

While both Cheyenne II and Laredo basses were made available in all of the color choices of the time, the Cheyenne IIs were also blessed with an additional selection of translucent clear colors: Trans Red, Trans Blue, and Trans Green. These rich tints were applied overall (not as a burst) and do not obscure the highly figured maple beneath. (See p. 131).

Five-strings

In 2002, Rickenbacker announced a new five-string version of the Cheyenne II, designating it the 4004Cii/5.

The new five-banger featured a wider neck and enlarged headstock to hold an additional tuner for the low B string, and HB-2 humbucking pickups as used on the 2020/2060 basses. Some users found reduced response from the outlying B and G strings with these pickups, and the company halted production of the Cii/5 until a redesign could be undertaken. It seems that only a few 4004Cii/5 basses were made in 2004. Accompanying the photo of a Cii/5 on the company brochure/poster is a cryptic "Also available as an eight string," but it doesn't appear that any eight-stringers were ever manufactured.

4004Cii/5 Cheyenne II Identifying Features

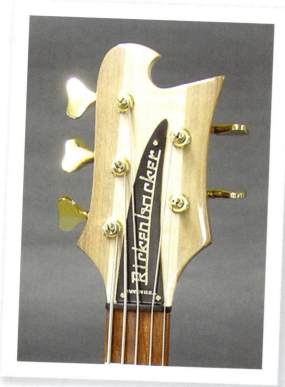

Elongated left side of headstock makes room for a fifth Schaller M4 tuner.

HB-2 pickups and a five-saddle ABM bridge were used on the Cii/5. Note this Mapleglo example has pickups in the lowered position.

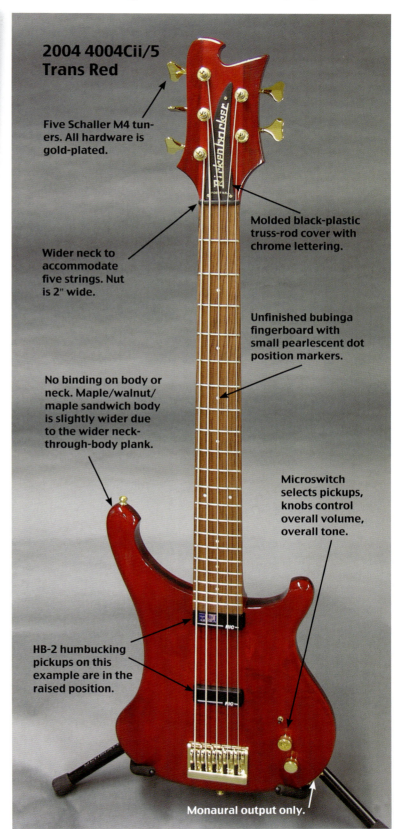

2004 4004Cii/5 Trans Red

Five Schaller M4 tuners. All hardware is gold-plated.

Molded black-plastic truss-rod cover with chrome lettering.

Wider neck to accommodate five strings. Nut is 2" wide.

Unfinished bubinga fingerboard with small pearlescent dot position markers.

No binding on body or neck. Maple/walnut/maple sandwich body is slightly wider due to the wider neck-through-body plank.

Microswitch selects pickups, knobs control overall volume, overall tone.

HB-2 humbucking pickups on this example are in the raised position.

Monaural output only.

4004LK "Lemmy"
Lemmy Kilmister Limited Edition
2000 – 2006

The 4004LK Lemmy Kilmister Limited Edition recognizes the hard-rocking bassist and vocalist of Motörhead (and earlier, Hawkwind) who has used Rickenbacker 4001 and 4003 basses for decades. Based on the 4004C Cheyenne bass, the LK features ornate, hand-carved oak leaves and acorns in bas-relief on the solid walnut body wings. Checker binding lined with white binding graces the edges of the flat-front body. The fingerboard is bound with white plastic. The neck-through-body center is maple, and the fingerboard is bubinga with large star position markers.

The Lemmy is the only Rickenbacker bass with three pickups, HB-1 humbuckers. Controls are like those on the other 4004 basses, but on the Lemmy, the three-way microswitch chooses either bass (neck) pickup, all pickups, or the center and treble (bridge) units. Gold-plated hardware includes the ABM tailpiece/ bridge, controls, and Schaller M4 tuners. The truss-rod cover is clear acrylic, back-painted with black lettering and gold background.

(Top) The spectacular "Lemmy." Graham Griffiths photo.
(Above) Lemmy Kilmister himself sports one of his own 4004LK basses in this RIC publicity photo.

(Below left) Resting in RIC's private museum, a prototype Lemmy exhibits a more shallow carving than production models. A third humbucking HB-1 pickup was added to production LKs. Erik Kutzler photo. (Below) Note the differences in leaf/acorn pattern and recessed areas between a 2003 Lemmy on the left, and a 2005 issue. No two 4004LKs are alike.

(Above) Luthier Richard Seccombe works on the last production run of Lemmy body wings in this 2005 shot. (Below) RIC CEO John Hall and Seccombe display Lemmy Kilmister's personal LK with its non-standard 4003 treble-pickup cover added as a handrest. Photos by Erik Kutzler.

Production

First announced on the official price sheet dated December 15, 1995, the new limited-edition bass retailed for $2,429. No mention was made on the list of the number to be produced. A run of 50 was planned, but this was later increased to 60 to fulfill orders. Although a two-pickup prototype was shown shortly after the announcement, it appears that the first-production Lemmy basses weren't issued until early in 2001.

The January 1, 1998, price sheet showed the Lemmy retailing for $2,799, but it was missing from the January 2000 price sheet. It reappeared on the January 2001 sheet, again at $2,799.

The on-again, off-again listing helps tell the tale of Lemmy production. The ornate carving on the face of the instrument had to be done by hand. The company assigned at least three carvers to the task, and with changes in personnel, production was sporadic. Most of the Lemmys came under the knife of the third and final artist, Richard Seccombe.

The individual treatment given to the Lemmys is easy to see when comparing the carving among several units. The pattern of oak leaves and acorns varies widely, as do the recessed areas for the carvings. Early Lemmys had the three pickups positioned closer together than later examples. Kilmister added a chrome-plated 4003 treble-pickup cover and bezel to his personal LK, preferring the convenience of a handrest, which the 4004 family basses normally do not provide.

The last Lemmys left the factory in 2006.

4004LK Lemmy Identifying Features

This 2001 Lemmy has the bass and treble pickups in the same positions as mid-production 4004L Laredo and 4004Cii Cheyenne II basses. The third pickup is centered between them. Tony D'Amico photo.

A closeup of the wood carving shows oak-leaf and acorn motif. Note the tiny rings in the background, produced by hammering a leather punch into the walnut. Graham Griffiths photo.

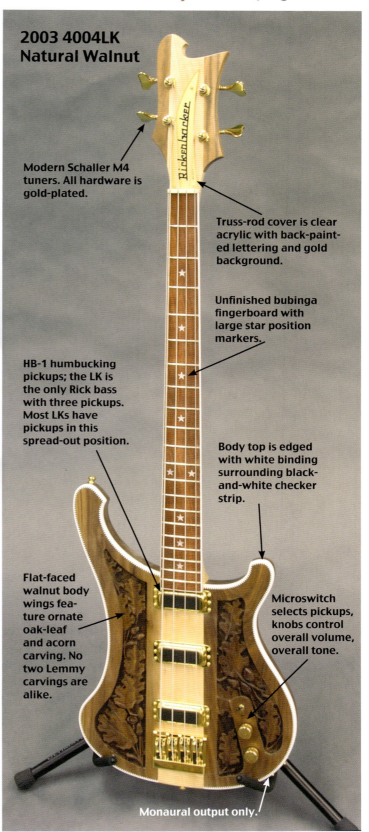

2003 4004LK Natural Walnut

Modern Schaller M4 tuners. All hardware is gold-plated.

Truss-rod cover is clear acrylic with back-painted lettering and gold background.

Unfinished bubinga fingerboard with large star position markers.

HB-1 humbucking pickups; the LK is the only Rick bass with three pickups. Most LKs have pickups in this spread-out position.

Body top is edged with white binding surrounding black-and-white checker strip.

Flat-faced walnut body wings feature ornate oak-leaf and acorn carving. No two Lemmy carvings are alike.

Microswitch selects pickups, knobs control overall volume, overall tone.

Monaural output only.

4001C64 & C64S
Sir Paul's bass times 2

2002 – 2011

Starting in 2002, Rickenbacker replaced the vintage V series with the new C series. (The significance of the "C" is known only to company management.) If the V series represented the instruments of the British Invasion, the C series zeroed in on the core of the movement: The Beatles. Following the lead of the "PMC" headstock option for lefty 4001V63 basses, the 4001C64 and 4001C64S replicates the appearance of one particular instrument at two important stages in its lifespan.

The C64

The 4001C64 replicates McCartney's lefty 4001S as given to him in 1964. Of course, this instrument was left-handed, but it had a right-handed neck, making the headstock look upside down. The C series bass offers that appearance – even for right-handed instruments! Equipped with the modern "reissue" Toaster-top and Horseshoe pickups and vintage-shaped pick guard, it also had a couple more changes from the previous V series. The tuning gears are made by Gotoh with "reversed" gears and small ferrules on the front of the headstock. A new tailpiece mounts with just three screws (underneath the bridge), and a tiny .0047µF (microfarad) capacitor is placed in line with the Horseshoe pickup's tone control.

The C64 was initially available in either Fireglo or Mapleglo but, like the V63, several examples in Jetglo appeared.

Some 4001C64 basses received a bright red shade of Fireglo as on this 2006 example.

(Above) Look familiar? Compare this 4001C64S with Paul McCartney's original bass on pp. 34 – 35. Lefty C64 basses are rare. Photo by Ian D. Martin via Peter Levett.

The C64S

The 4001C64S represents that same bass as it appeared in the mid-1970s. By then it had gone through a crazy psychedelic paint job, brutal stripping, and rough sanding that McCartney had inflicted. During a quick stint in rehab at the factory, RIC had replaced a dead Horseshoe pickup and added a newer-style surround, replaced the tailpiece, and did a general cleaning and tuneup.

To make the 4001C64S look like McCartney's Wings-era bass, the factory knocked down the sharp corners of the "cresting wave" body horns and applied a clear, silky-smooth satin finish – unique to the C64S.

(Left) Seeing double? Not quite! Note the sharp corners of the body's cresting wave horns on the 2006 4001C64 in glossy Jetglo on the left. The same color graces a 2004 4001C64S with its rounded-off horns and zero fret. Also notice the more modern treble-pickup surround and five-screw tailpiece of the C64S.

More colors appear

As on the V63 bass, the factory started experimenting with different finishes near the end of C-series bass production. As early as 2004, C64 and C64S basses were seen in glossy Jetglo, and at least one C64S has been observed in glossy Fireglo. In 2009, several C64S basses were dressed in a gorgeous satin black – and then at least one was discovered in satin Fireglo!

The one remaining standard RIC color of the period, Midnight Blue, was not to be left out, and examples of that rich metallic dark blue have been seen on both C64 and C64S basses. Even a satin version of Midnight Blue was applied to a few C64Ss.

RIC stopped taking orders for the C64 and C64S in January 2009, but production to fulfill orders continued through 2011.

Early in 2010, the factory produced a limited run of 60 Fireglo basses based on the C64, but with the headstock turned back to the normal style. A clear acrylic "tug bar" was attached to the pick guard for an added vintage touch. This run was made specially for the 60th anniversary of Shinseido, a Japanese vendor, and was advertised as the "Model 1999 Fireglo – Limited Edition." The "1999" harks back to the model number applied to the famous 4001S basses that England's Rose-Morris ordered in the 1960s.

Late in 2011, a special order for 15 C64 basses resulted in five each finished in White, "Sea Foam Green," and "TV Yellow."

(Below left) A C64S in satin Fireglo. Photo by Chris Clayton/Pick of the Ricks. (Below) A C64S in glossy Fireglo. Photo by International Vintage Guitars. (Bottom) Beautiful Midnight Blue was applied to this C64S. Ron O'Keefe photo. (Below right) One of the special "Model 1999" basses bound for Japan. Note the "normal" headstock and added tug bar.

4001C64S Identifying Features

Both C64 and C64S basses have reversed headstock with upside-down "smiley" clear-acrylic truss-rod cover. Note small tuner ferrules.

Vintage models feature a squared-off neck heel.

C64S basses simulate Paul McCartney's overzealous sanding and reshaping of the crested-wave body horns of his original 4001S.

2003 4001C64S Clear Satin

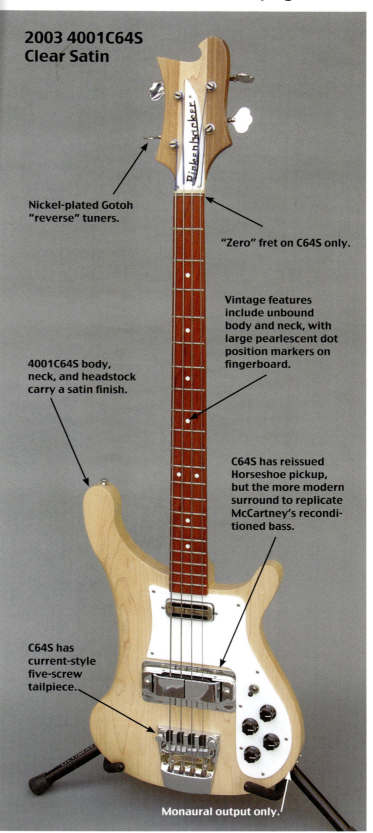

Nickel-plated Gotoh "reverse" tuners.

"Zero" fret on C64S only.

Vintage features include unbound body and neck, with large pearlescent dot position markers on fingerboard.

4001C64S body, neck, and headstock carry a satin finish.

C64S has reissued Horseshoe pickup, but the more modern surround to replicate McCartney's reconditioned bass.

C64S has current-style five-screw tailpiece.

Monaural output only.

Finishes

Standard and special colors

As with most modern guitar manufacturers, the range of available colors Rickenbacker has offered varies from narrow to wide and back again, with some colors limited to certain models, and others restricted into narrow timeframes.

There have been several chemical formula changes to finishes over the years, too. Rickenbacker's clear coats are not "nitro" finishes, but catalyzed coatings known as "conversion varnish." New UV-cured formulas were introduced in 2010, speeding the curing time of the varnish.

Mapleglo (or Natural)
1957 to present

Like Rickenbacker bass production, the availability of finish options started slowly. When the Model 4000 bass was introduced in 1957, it was offered only in a "natural" finish highlighting the solid woods underneath a clear sealer coat. Historically, this is the only "color" that has been offered continuously since then. "Natural" was renamed "Mapleglo" (MG) in the late 1960s.

Environmental conditions yellow the clear varnish over time. These include UV exposure, cigarette smoke and other pollutants, and possibly chemical reactions to the wood and the metal and plastic parts.

Usually, Mapleglo basses are fitted with the standard white binding and plastic parts and chrome hardware. For a time (1986 – 1992), Mapleglo

Heading upstairs are 4003 basses from the author's collection in several "Color of the Year" shades. From bottom, 2000 COY Sea Green, 2001 COY Desert Gold, 2002 COY Burgundy, 2003 – 04 COY Montezuma Brown, and 2006 COY Amber Fireglo.

basses came standard with black trim – binding, pick guard, and truss-rod cover (TRC) – and black hardware – tuners, pickup surrounds, tailpiece, and strap pins. During that time, they could be ordered with the old standard white and chrome trim for a "reverse trim" upcharge.

The "ambering" of the clear varnish is best seen on Mapleglo. The 4001C64 (right) is a 2003 model, while the 4001 (far right) was finished in 1969.

Fireglo
1960 to present

The second "evergreen" color is Rickenbacker's signature "Fireglo" red burst. First known as "Fireglow," Fireglo (FG) is a translucent red applied in a burst pattern, lightly (or not at all) in the center of the burst, building to a deep red, sometimes nearly to black, on the edges of the body, headstock, and neck. The paint itself dries to a flat sheen, and the final finish is built up with multiple coats of clear gloss.

Fireglo is nearly always paired with white binding and plastic parts and chrome- or nickel-plated hardware.

Fireglo has a wide variance in application, and it is thought that particularly heavy applications of Fireglo were offered as "Autumnglo" in the 1960s. The clear coat over Fireglo yellows over time, and part of the wide variance can be credited to the individual finisher as well.

Instruments painted in the mid-2000s were notable for their sometimes concentrated edge application and light overspray toward the center. These basses appear almost pink in the middle. Later in the 2000s and into the 2010s, the bursts were more gradual, resembling instruments of the 1960s and '70s.

This pair of 4001C64 basses from August 2006 (left) and July 2005 shows how variable the application of Fireglo can be. Ron O'Keefe photo.

Jetglo
1963 to present

The last of the three "evergreen" colors is Jetglo. First known as "Black Diamond," the gloss-black finish is made from solid black paint and multiple coats of clear gloss. Jetglo (JG) is often applied to cover

Fine examples of Jetglo on a 1967 roundtop 4005 (near right) and a 1973 4001.

unattractive or flawed wood grain. Older examples of Jetglo sometimes have a greenish cast due to the yellowing of the clear coat.

Jetglo usually comes with white binding and plastic and chrome- or nickel-plated hardware, but there are many examples where the "reverse trim" option was chosen. There are some examples that show a factory overcoat of Jetglo finish on the

(Right) The 4001C64S in satin black. Olivia's Vintage photo.

already-attached white binding to attain the "reverse trim" condition.

In 2007, a few 4003 basses appeared in a very dark gray version of Jetglo. This experiment was produced by applying a white-tinted clear gloss coat over the Jetglo. Some collectors have dubbed this finish "Grayglo."

Several 4001C64S basses near the end of that model's production were finished in black with a smooth, clear satin overcoat.

A 1971 4003 in "Eggplantglo," the very dark version of Burgundy.

Burgundy was resurrected as "Color of the Year" for 2002, here on a 4003.

Burgundy
Mid-1960s to '84, 2002 to '03

Burgundy (occasionally listed as "Burgundyglo") is an overall application of translucent red-wine color. The hue varied over the years from a bright cherry color to a very deep maroon. This dark application appeared on some 4001 instruments in the 1970 to '72 period and has been dubbed "Eggplantglo" by some collectors.

Burgundy came standard with white binding and plastic, and chrome- or nickel-plated hardware.

Burgundy (BG) was available as a standard finish starting in the mid-1960s and continuing until 1984. It resurfaced as the "Color of the Year" for 2002, so basses could be ordered in Burgundy in that calendar year. Production to fulfill orders carried into 2003.

A restored 1972 4001 in Azureglo.

Azureglo
Late 1960s to 1985

Azureglo (AZ) was the first "blue" to be applied to Rickenbacker basses, starting as early as 1968 and continuing until 1985 when it was replaced by Midnight Blue. Azureglo is not translucent or metallic, but a solid medium blue paint ranging from a slightly greenish hue to a deep Navy blue. According to Paul Wilczynski, an accomplished Ricken-

backer restorer, Azureglo was initially based on a Volkswagen color, formula L360 Sea Blue. Paul also indicates that Azureglo became bluer and somewhat darker as it aged.

Azureglo was fitted with white binding and plastic, and chrome- or nickel-plated hardware.

Azureglo Rickenbacker 4001 basses became quite the rage when one appeared in the centerfold of the February 1977 issue of *Playboy* magazine, held by Playmate and Gene Simmons (Kiss) associate Star Stowe.

Autumnglo/Walnut
Mid-1960s to early 1985

The story of Autumnglo and Walnut is complex. Legend has it that, in the 1960s, "Autumnglow" was simply a name given to darker applications of Fireglo; that is difficult to document. Price sheets from the mid-1960s mention "Autumnglow" (with the w) as being available on some guitar models, but these same sheets list the only colors available for basses as being Mapleglo and Fireglo. There were a few brown-burst basses in the late 1950s, but in those days anything the customer wanted was accomplished.

It appears dedicated shaded-brown "Autumnglo" basses began to appear in early 1973. Things get complicated from there, though. Several basses from 1974-'76 were finished in translucent brown overall instead of a burst. The shade of Autumnglo also varied from a warm red brown to a darker greenish brown.

In the late-'70s, RIC complicated matters by listing both "Autumnglo (ATG) matte brown" and "Walnut (WAL) brown" as custom colors. These price sheets also list "Matte brown (BRN)" as a standard color for 3000 and 3001 model basses. Examination of dozens of instruments and photos shows plenty of burst and overall translucent brown 3001 basses. Many late-'70s and early-'80s 4001 basses display a satin clear coat; presumably these are "Autumn-glo matte brown," while others are glossy, apparently "Walnut brown."

Listing of Autumnglo as an available custom color continued to the 1980 price sheet, but is absent in 1981. Walnut in the 1981 sheet was described as "shaded brown" and appears that way in price sheets through 1984. The last Walnut basses were finished in early 1985. Some Autumnglo/Walnut basses were assembled with black body binding and black-plastic pick guard and truss-rod covers.

(Below left) A 1976 4001 in overall translucent brown. (Below) A 1978 Autumnglo 4001 paired with a 1981 Walnut 4001. Note the Walnut bass has black binding on the body.

White
Early 1970s to 1999

White (WHT) began to appear on Rickenbacker basses around 1972, and was often accompanied by contrasting black binding on the 4001 body wings (retaining white binding on the neck), a black plastic pick guard, and a reverse-painted clear acrylic truss-rod cover (white lettering with black background). Some early examples had the black or white outer binding enclosing inner checker binding. White was considered a "custom" color, and the factory tacked an extra charge onto orders.

From 1981 to 1983, RIC price sheets advised "White color is not covered under warranty." This may have been in response to some buyers' chagrin when the clear coat over the pristine White finish yellowed within a few years' time.

From the mid-1980s, White 4003 basses also had black binding on the neck to match that of the body. This addition occurred around the time of the introduction of blackened hardware, which also became standard on White basses. A purchaser could always opt for "reverse trim" for an upcharge, so there are a few White instruments with white/chrome trim.

White was removed from the finish palette in 1999.

A 1998 4003 in White with white trim.

An early 1980s 4003 in the first version of Ruby

RIC reintroduced Ruby in 2012, here on a 4004L Laredo. Jeff Scott photo.

Ruby
1981 to '89, 2012 to present

Ruby (RBY) was the first "metallic" color in Rickenbacker's color palette. A brilliant red metallic, the first version of Ruby was produced by applying clear red over a metallic silver base coat. This "candy color" method was typical of paints applied to automobiles. Later on, a new one-step metallic red formula was used for Ruby.

Ruby came standard with white/chrome trim, but examples of "reverse trim" exist with black binding, plastic, and hardware.

Ruby was dropped in 1989, but was reintroduced in 2012 and remains a stock color.

Midnight Blue
1985 to present

Midnight Blue (MID) became RIC's standard blue in 1985, taking over from the discontinued Azureglo. While Azureglo was a solid medium blue, Midnight Blue is a fine-grained metallic that has varied in hue and intensity over the years. Early on, Midnight Blue was a "candy color" – a translucent blue sprayed over a metallic silver undercoat. Later on, a silica-based solid metallic paint was developed.

Varying with paint source, batch, and application, Midnight Blue can be a vivid blue, dark blue, and even slightly purple, but always shows the specular reflections characteristic of metallic paints.

From 1986 through 1998, basses finished in Midnight Blue came standard with black trim and hardware. White/chrome trim became standard on MID basses in 1999.

Midnight Blue continues as a standard color.

(Far left) a 2003 4003. (Upper left) A 1989 4003 with then-standard black trim and hardware. (Left) Satin Midnight Blue applied to a late-production 4001C64S. Ron O'Keefe photos.

A 1985 4003 with the stock black trim and hardware. Olivia's Vintage photo.

A 1985 Red 4003 with black trim and hardware.

Cream was applied only to the 4001CS Chris Squire Limited Edition.

Silver
1985 to '89

Silver (SIL) was a very fine-grained silver metallic available from 1985 to 1989. Silver came standard with black trim and hardware, but examples with "reverse trim" (white/chrome) have been found. Silver was likely used as the base coat for the early "candy color" style mixes of Midnight Blue and Ruby. Many examples of Silver Rickenbackers take on a green tint as the clear overcoat yellows over time.

Red
1985 to '98

Started in 1985 and coming standard with black trim and hardware, Red (RED) was a solid, bright, fire-engine red (non-metallic). It could be ordered with white trim and chrome hardware for an upcharge, and a few examples of this "reverse trim" exist. Red was available through 1998.

Cream
4001CS only
1990 to 2000

A special cream color was developed for the 4001CS Chris Squire Limited Edition basses made from 1990 to 2000. This simulated the finish that Squire had applied to the 4001S (Rose-Morris 1999) that he has played for decades. Sometimes the clear coat on Cream yellows, and under some fluorescent lights, Cream appears to take on a greenish tinge.

Turquoise
1994 to 2003

Turquoise (TUR) is an attractive metallic blue-green (some call it "teal") that appears differently in varying light. Under incandescent light, it appears to be a rich metallic green, while in sunlight, it appears to be a metallic greenish blue.

Turquoise came standard with white trim and chrome hardware. Reverse trim was an option during the time period when Turquoise was available, but this author has not found any examples with black trim. Turquoise was dropped from Rickenbacker's color choices after 2003.

Turquoise 4004 looks good with gold!

2002 4003 with custom pick guard.

Sea Green
2000 to '01

The first of RIC's "Color of the Year" program, Sea Green (SG) is a vivid aquamarine color, dissimilar from other manufacturer's less-saturated "sea foam" colors. Sea Green was available for instruments ordered during the calendar year of 2000, so some received 2001 date serial numbers when completed. Apparently, Sea Green generated few orders, so not many basses were finished in this color. Most examples found are the deluxe 4003 basses, but a few 4001V63 vintage models, and at least one 4003S/5, were finished in Sea Green. This author has not found any Sea Green 4004 basses, nor any with the "reverse trim" option (black hardware, binding, plastic).

Sea Green Ricks are rare, so spotting a 4003 and 4001V63 together is an event!

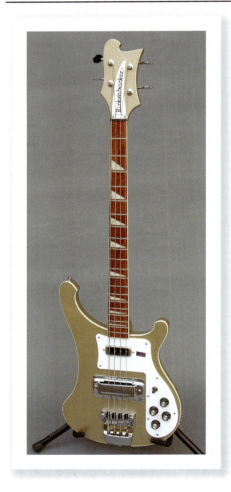

(Left) A Desert Gold 4003 in standard trim. (Above) A few Desert Gold basses were built with black trim and hardware. Chris Harris photo.

Desert Gold
2001 to '02

Not a brilliant, sparkly gold, but a soft, metallic tan, Desert Gold (DG) became the second shade in the "Color of the Year" program. Desert Gold could be specified for instruments ordered in the 2001 calendar year, and production stretched into 2002. Several basses in Desert Gold were manufactured with "reverse trim" (black hardware, binding, plastic), and a 4004L Laredo in DG has been documented. There are also sightings of 4003S/5 and 4003S/8 basses in Desert Gold.

Montezuma Brown
2003 to '06

Rickenbacker's return to a brown-burst finish was Montezuma Brown (MB). It was so popular that it became the only shade in the "Color of the Year" program to be officially extended; customers could order MB in both 2003 and 2004, and production to fulfill orders extended into 2006. "Monte" shows some variation, ranging from a pleasing, strong ice-tea reddish brown to applications where the outer edges appear nearly black. The only Rickenbacker bass models found in this color are the deluxe 4003, 4004L Laredo, and 4004Cii Cheyenne II.

A 2005 4004Cii in the dark-edged variety of Montezuma Brown.

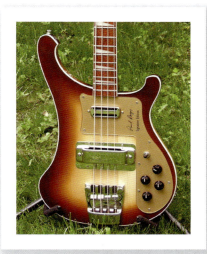

The author's 2004 4003 shows off the lighter shade and a custom pick guard.

Blue Boy
2002 to '06

Blue Boy (BB), a soft powder blue, was clearly a salute to the refinished Rickenbacker instruments used by "Gentleman Jim" Reeves and the Blue Boys in the early 1960s. The first production Blue Boy instruments were ordered by a retailer in the U.K. and delivered in 2002 to '03. RIC chose Blue Boy as the "Color of the Year" for 2004 (along with Montezuma Brown's second year). Orders were fulfilled into early 2006. Most Blue Boy basses were deluxe 4003 models, but a few 4004L Laredo and 4004Cii Cheyenne IIs also were made. In some cases, the clear coat yellows, giving a minty greenish tint to the Blue Boy.

A 2004 4003 deluxe bass in Blue Boy.

Blueburst
2005 to '09

"Color of the Year" for 2005 was Blueburst (BBR), a brilliant translucent blue applied in a "burst" pattern. Blueburst turned out to be one of the most popular COY choices. Most 4003 basses finished in Blueburst were produced from 2005 to '07, while most 4004L Laredo and 4004Cii Cheyenne II models were produced in 2008.

A pair of Blueburst basses: A 4003 and a 4004Cii Cheyenne II.

The amber-tinted clear coat is best seen on the binding of the deluxe 4003.

Amber Fireglo
2006 to '08

The last in Rickenbacker's "Color of the Year" program was Amber Fireglo (AFG), a purposely aged version of Fireglo. A tinted clear coat did the trick, simulating Fireglo that appears yellowed by time and exposure. The yellowed clear coat is especially evident on the white binding on the deluxe 4003. Examples of 4004L Laredo and 4004Cii Cheyenne II were also finished in Amber Fireglo. RIC CEO John Hall said that AFG was the most successful in the "Color of the Year" program, and production of instruments drifted into 2008. Rickenbacker discontinued the "Color of the Year" series and announced no new color for 2007, preferring to concentrate on production of the standard colors to reduce the (by then) two-year backlog in orders.

Dark Cherry Metallic
2006 to '07

While not a "Color of the Year," Dark Cherry Metallic (DCM) was chosen for Rickenbacker's commemorative 75th anniversary issue instruments in 2006. This deep, black-cherry metallic paint exhibits the fine grain of Rickenbacker's other metallic paints and is complemented by gold back-painted clear acrylic pick guard and truss-rod cover, both specially laser-etched for the occasion. Only 75 deluxe 4003 basses were issued in the special edition, manufactured in the closing months of the anniversary year and extending into early 2007.

The 75th Anniversary 4003 in Dark Cherry Metallic.

Cheyenne II special colors
2000 to present

Special, vivid see-through colors restricted to the 4004Cii Cheyenne II basses were introduced when that model became available. Trans Blue, Trans Red, and Trans Green are tinted clear coats applied overall to the

(From Left) 4004Cii Cheyenne II basses in Trans Blue, Trans Red (Mike Parks / The Music Connection photo), and Trans Green.

instruments (except for the fingerboards), allowing the attractive wood grain underneath to show through.

Oiled Walnut finish
1992 to '99 and 2001 to '06

Not really a "color" this time, but a finish of sorts. The debut of Rickenbacker's 4004C Cheyenne (and companion 650S Sierra and 650D Dakota guitars) in 1992 introduced beautiful walnut body and headstock wings with no obscuring paint. Instruments received an application of Watco Danish Oil for a "rubbed-oil finish." The 4004C Cheyenne basses were made this way from 1992 to 1999 when they were superseded by the mostly varnished-maple 4004Cii Cheyenne II. The exposed-walnut treatment returned, however, with the 60 special 4004LK Lemmy Kilmister Limited Editions made between 2001 and 2006.

A 4004LK "Lemmy" in Oiled Walnut finish shows off its oak-leaf and acorn carvings while resting among real oak leaves.

Customs, mods,
Letting that freak flag fly

So far, this book has illustrated the factory standard models and finishes. But there is more to see. Plenty of Rick bass players and collectors put their own personal touches on their instruments, either by doing it themselves or engaging professional refinishers and luthiers.

Some Rick owners modify their instruments to their liking by swapping out pickups or electronics. Some add to or rearrange strings, and some even built entirely new instruments using Rick bass components. Still others transfigure their basses with custom paint jobs or create retro instruments from current basses. Enjoy the eye candy!

(Right) Brian Crisman's custom bass started life as a 4004L Laredo, then received an overall black finish (on the fingerboard, too, with "pin-dot" position markers ala the "Blackstar"), blackened hardware, supplemental electronics, and a subtle green flame over the body.

and one-offs

"Aquabass" is the nickname given to Russ Rubman's spectacular 4001C64. The reef and shark motif was created with mother-of-pearl inlays. Photos by Thomas Decker via Russ Rubman.

(Left) While we're on that Aqua thing, here's Kira Moon's custom refinished 2030 in aqua burst.

(Right) Both sides of Erik Kutzler's "blue flame Rick," a custom painted Jetglo 4001 from 1975.

(Left) Incorporating bits of 50+ years of Rickenbacker basses, this tribute started life as a Fireglo 4004L Laredo. The pick guard salutes the original design of the 4000 bass, and the pickup layout is similar to that of the 4002. John Luke Photography.

(Above and right) A custom built double-neck bass made from 3000 and 3001 parts. The second neck features E, A, and D paired octaves. Dane Wilder photos.

(Above) A detail of the "Scarab" bass, an amazing refinish of a 4003 Shadow once owned by the late Gary Strater of Starcastle. Photo from Kevin Lange.

(Left) It would take a thousand words to describe Mark Walker's handpainted lefty (played righty) 4001. Good thing there are photos!

If you're a fan of black trim with a lot of maple, this is the bass for you. Larry Davis stripped the aging white paint off of a 4003SPC Tuxedo from the author's collection, applied a satin clear coat, and revealed a "Naked Tux."

(Above) Kenny Howes' round-top 4005 refinished in deep translucent green.

(Left) Dane Wilder's shout-out to Chris Squire and his eight-string prototype. This 4001V63 received a new "potato-head" headstock to hold octave strings and a refinish in Squire's cream paint job.

(Right) The author's '72 4001 received a "berry burst" refinish. The resoration was done by Ted Staberow and Paul Wilczynski.

(Below) Another wild one from Dane Wilder, a new Midnight Blue 4003 with a reissue Horseshoe pickup, two HB-1 humbuckers, and a little extra nod to Lemmy Kilmister. Dane Wilder photo.

Look a little odd to you? It's a factory one-off, lefty, short-scale 4003S. Photo by Ian D. Martin via Peter Levett.

(Above) Dane Wilder replaced the humbucking pickups with two Toaster-tops, added a pick guard and control harness, and produced a 4003S/4004 hybrid.

(Left) Dale Fortune refinished this once-Fireglo 4001V63 in White with a dark-stained fingerboard and headstock wings.

(Right) Several luthiers have found the four-string 4004 basses ideal platforms for a five-string conversion. This Cheyenne II has a volume/volume/tone mod as well as Hipshot Ultralite tuners with clover-leaf keys.

137

Rickenbacker produced several one-off basses and sold them on eBay. This flamed maple top 4003 was the most spectacular of the specials. The back (above) reveals walnut body wings and a thick walnut strip down the middle of the neck-through-body assembly. RIC photos.

A couple more specials from RIC. (Left) Dubbed "Whiskeyglo," this overall honey brown finish adorns a 4003. (Above) This special vintage-syle bass features a tobacco-burst finish along with black trim and hardware. RIC photos.

Near the end of 4001C64 production, RIC finished five each in special colors for a special order. From left are "Sea Foam Green," White, and "T.V. Yellow." Olivia's Vintage photos.

Controls and adjustments

Like any typical bass guitar, a Rickenbacker has the usual features: strings, tuners, pickups, volume and tone controls, and an output jack. But some features on a Rickenbacker are different from the others. I mean, what is this "Rick-O-Sound" thing, and where is the mute? A quick illustrated tutorial is in order.

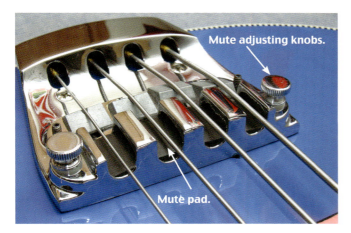

Rickenbacker tailpiece/bridge.

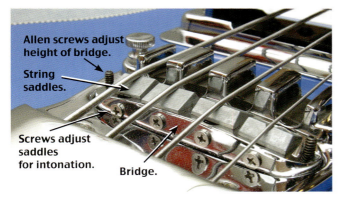

Tailpiece and bridge

Rickenbacker's classic cast-metal tailpiece is a multifunctional cornerstone of most models. It serves as the string anchor and a holder for the bridge and mute assemblies. The two large thumbscrews on either side of the mute cover thread into the mute base plate, and turning them raises and lowers the foam-rubber mute.

The bridge assembly is a separate piece that rests in the depression right behind the mute. An Allen screw on either side is used to adjust the height of the bridge, which affects the instrument's "action." Four metal saddles rest in slots on the top of the bridge and are adjusted for intonation with Phillips screws that move the saddles fore and aft in the slots.

The tailpiece/bridge assemblies used on the 2000-series and 4004 basses are simpler affairs, but don't offer a mute. The ABM and Schaller bridges have rolling saddles for side-to-side spacing, tiny Allen screws for individual string height, and spring-loaded screws for intonation.

ABM tailpiece/bridge (4004 series).

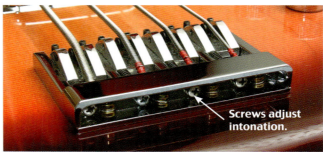

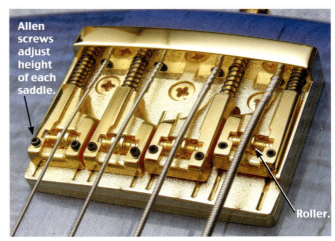

Schaller tailpiece/bridge (2000 series, late 4004 series).

Pickup height adjustment

The mounting system for the treble (bridge) pickup (Horseshoe or High-gain) is another characteristic Rickenbacker design. The pickup is mounted to a base plate that has two holes tapped for large height-adjusting screws. If assembled properly, the plastic cover on the High-gain pickup floats with the pickup when adjusted for height.

The bass (neck) pickup (Toaster or High-gain) is mounted to the plastic pick guard and is adjusted for height with two small screws that thread into the pickup's mounting ring. Small rubber grommets provide some spring and cushion and help keep the pickup from cracking the pick guard if improperly adjusted.

In addition to overall pickup height, late model High-gain pickups also feature individual pole height adjustment with the use of an Allen wrench.

Pickup height on the 2000-series basses is adjusted from the back with pairs of Allen screws set in holes drilled through the body.

On the 4004 basses, both Humbucking pickups are mounted on foam cushions set in shallow depressions routed into the top of the body, and adjusted by turning small wood screws that go through the pickup mounting rings.

Large screws adjust pickup height.

Horseshoe or High-gain treble pickup.

Screws adjust pickup height.

Toaster-top or High-gain bass pickup.

Middle screws adjust pickup height.

HB-1 Humbucking pickup on 4004.

Truss rods

Perhaps the biggest bugaboo with Rickenbacker basses has been maladjustment of the neck and truss rods. Most problems stem from users and technicians not understanding how the pair of "hairpin" truss rods (found in pre-1986 basses) work.

Unlike traditional truss rods which can "move" the neck when adjusted, the hairpin rods were used to "set" the neck after it is moved manually. These "old style" rods were made from flat steel stock, threaded for an adjustment nut at one end, clipped to a chisel point at the other, and then folded mid-length to bring the ends close together. The threaded end of each rod is about an inch longer and fits through a hole drilled in a metal thrust plate positioned in the cavity in the headstock (or at the body end of the neck on early 4003 basses). Long hexagonal standoff nuts (¼" 10-32) are used for adjustment.

When the nut is tightened, the threaded end is drawn out, but the chiseled end stops against the metal thrust plate, causing the folded rod to bow slightly. This makes the rod work like a spring, counteracting undesirable bowing of the neck.

Proper adjustment of the early-style rods relies on the user's understanding that the neck should be forced into

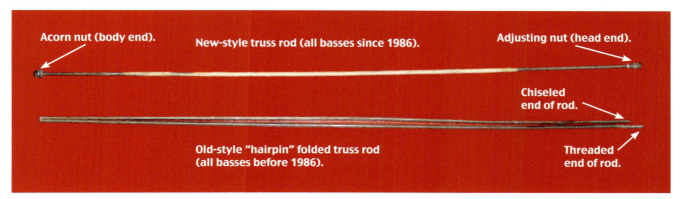

Acorn nut (body end).

New-style truss rod (all basses since 1986).

Adjusting nut (head end).

Chiseled end of rod.

Old-style "hairpin" folded truss rod (all basses before 1986).

Threaded end of rod.

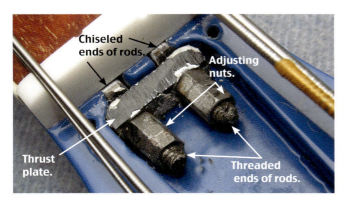

Chiseled ends of rods.

Adjusting nuts.

Thrust plate.

Threaded ends of rods.

Old-style truss-rod adjusters in headstock cavity.

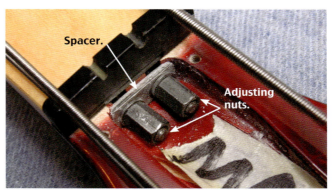

Spacer.

Adjusting nuts.

Current truss-rod adjusters in headstock cavity.

the desired condition by hand, and then the nuts tightened to lock the rod into the new condition. Things go wrong when the technician tries the traditional method of moving the neck by tightening the rods alone. This usually results in bent rod ends, broken rods, cracked necks, or separated fingerboards.

Starting in 1986, Rickenbacker ditched the hairpin truss-rod design, opting to go with the more traditional style rod. The new rods (used on all basses from 1986 onward) are made from $\frac{5}{32}$" round steel rod stock cut a little longer than the fingerboard. One end of each rod is anchored to the body end of a trough with a star washer and acorn nut. Thin strips of wood are fit into the truss channels establishing a gentle arc to each rod. At the

head end, the rods take ¼" 8-32 threaded hex standoff nuts for adjustments.

The new-style rods are capable of moving the neck into position, but manually moving the neck and then tightening the nuts is always safer – and easier. In all cases, adjusting the truss rods should be done in small steps (one eighth or one quarter turn of the nuts) and allowing the neck to acclimate to its new position for a day or so before more adjustment is applied.

To prevent users from overstressing the truss adjustment, RIC recommends (and offers for sale) the Xcelite L8 ¼" nut driver that fits all Rickenbacker truss-rod adjustment nuts.

Rick-O-Sound

Oh, and that extra output jack on most deluxe Rickenbacker basses? Just what is "Rick-O-Sound"? This separate output is wired so that each pickup can transmit its signal through separate wires (in a special stereo cable) and then out to two amplifiers or two channels of an amplification system. This way, the player can dial in a certain tone from the bass pickup, and a separate and distinct tone from the treble pickup and have them projected to the listeners through separate speakers for an ideal mix.

Rick-O-Sound was an option on the deluxe 4001 bass until the late 1960s when it became a standard item. It remains standard for the deluxe 4003 basses. It is usually

not fitted to the down-trimmed S and vintage models, 2000 series basses, 3000, 3001, or 4004 basses. It was installed on the recording 4002, and some (but not all) hollow-body 4005 basses.

Rickenbacker date codes

Radio-Tel and Rickenbacker have used an alphanumeric method of registering instruments since the beginning of bass production. The system of letters and numbers changed several times over the years, so dating a bass can be confusing. In all cases, though, the serials are stamped into either the jack plate, the base plate of the bridge (on early 4000 models), or on the neck-bolt plate found on 3000- and 2000-series basses.

In the late 1950s, the 4000-model basses had serial identifiers starting with B (for bass), then the first digit (standing for the last number of the year) along with a sequential serial number. So a 1957 Model 4000 bass would start with B7, followed by a three-digit number. According to Richard R. Smith's *The Complete Guide To Rickenbacker Guitars* (Centerstream Publishing, 1987) the "first" registered bass was coded B7100. (Why the sequential number started with 100 instead of 001 is anyone's guess.) Following this system, the second registered bass would have been coded B7101. So in 1958, the codes would read B8xxx (x for serials). Example **1** shows the jackplate from a 4000 bass. The code (B9139) indicates

1959 and was the 139th Rickenbacker bass made.

The system was changed slightly in November 1960. The B was replaced by a letter that stood for the year. For the last two months of 1960 only, the letter J started the code (J is the tenth letter in the alphabet) indicating the last digit of 1960. This was followed by a second letter indicating the month. November 1960 instruments would have JK codes (K is the eleventh letter), so December 1960 would show JL.

1961 – 1986 numbering system First character is year, second is month

Year code	A	B	C	D	E	F	G	H	I	J	K	L	M
Year	1961	1962	1963	1964	1965	1966	1967	1968	1969	1970	1971	1972	1973
Year code	N	O	P	Q	R	S	T	U	V	W	X	Y	Z
Year	1974	1975	1976	1977	1978	1979	1980	1981	1982	1983	1984	1985	1986

Month code	A	B	C	D	E	F	G	H	I	J	K	L
Month	Jan	Feb	Mar	Apr	May	Jun	July	Aug	Sep	Oct	Nov	Dec

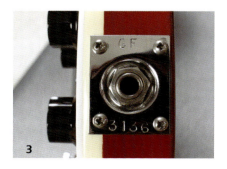

The system started over again in 1961 with the first letter representing the year and a second letter representing the month. This date code stood apart from the rest of the serial, usually at the top of the jack plate with the rest of the serial at the bottom. At this point, the serial numbers appear to identify a sequence of production during the year. January 1961 basses were coded AA, February 1961 AB, and so on. In 1962, the codes started with BA; 1963, CA; and onward. Example **2** shows a

March 1961 code (AC209) stamped on the bridge plate of a 4000 bass. Example **3** is from a 4001 bass made in June 1967. This system was used through December 1986, when the codes read ZL.

It is possible that a serial on a bass made in November or December 1970 would duplicate one from the last two months of 1960. But the style and shape of the early 4000 (the only bass model available in 1960) could never be mistaken for one of the later models.

1987 – 1996 numbering system First character is month, second is year

Month code	A	B	C	D	E	F	G	H	I	J	K	L
Month	Jan	Feb	Mar	Apr	May	Jun	July	Aug	Sep	Oct	Nov	Dec

Year code	0	1	2	3	4	5	6	7	8	9
Year	1987	1988	1989	1990	1991	1992	1993	1994	1995	1996

Having run out of letters, RIC modified the coding system in 1987. This time, the month represented by a letter comes first (A for January through L for December), followed by a single number representing the year (0 indicating 1987, 1 for 1988, and so on). Example **4** shows the date code and serial applied to the black-painted neck plate on a Fireglo 2060 El Dorado made in November 1992 (K54183). Example **5** is the gold-plated jackplate of a 4004C Cheyenne made in May 1993 (E67806).

1997 – November 1998 numbering system First character is month, second is year

Month code	M	N	P	Q	R	S	T	U	V	W	X	Y
Month	Jan	Feb	Mar	Apr	May	Jun	July	Aug	Sep	Oct	Nov	Dec

Year code	0	1
Year	1997	1998

It was back to 0 for 1997, but to avoid duplicating serials from the previous 10 years, the month codes were changed to letters from M through Y (not using O). An October 1998 bass would be coded W1. This system lasted until November 1998, when the present system was initiated. Example **6** is a jackplate from a Fireglo 4004L Laredo made in November 1997 (X04431).

Current numbering system

Starting in December 1998 a simpler date-coding system was established. The last two digits of the year stand alone – no more letters – with a five- or six-digit number representing the serial; the first two numbers indicating the week of manufacture. Example **7** shows the jackplate of a 2007 Dark Cherry Metallic 75th Anniversary 4003 (0711515) made the 11th week of 2007 (the middle week of March, in this case), and the last three digits indicating that particular instrument as it came off the assembly line.

If there is a weakness in the registration system, it is that the serials are stamped onto easily removed and exchanged metal parts. Lately, the serial number is usually duplicated in ink inside the instrument's control cavity, example **8**, here on a Montezuma Brown 4003 from 2004.

About the author

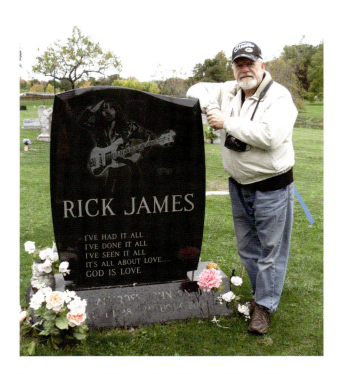

Know of a more fitting end to this book? The author pays respects to the Buffalo, New York, gravesite of James Ambrose Johnson, Jr., AKA Rick James. The headstone features a photo-engraving of James complete with a Rickenbacker 4001. Photo by Susan Boyer Fischer.

Paul D. Boyer is a retired magazine editor and photographer and, obviously, a Rickenbacker bass enthusiast. Originally from Buffalo, New York, Paul and his wife, Dorothy, live in Wisconsin, not far from Milwaukee. He is a U.S. Air Force veteran, serving four years as a still photographer and combat cameraman. After a career as Senior Editor for *FineScale Modeler* magazine (Kalmbach Publishing Co.) for 24 years, Paul retired and started work on *The Rickenbacker Electric Bass* in 2006.

Paul continues to build museum-quality static scale aircraft models for his private collection, for publications, and for several clients. His work is on display at the Experimental Aircraft Association AirVenture Museum in Oshkosh, Wisconsin; the National Naval Aviation Museum in Pensacola, Florida; the National Museum of the USAF in Dayton, Ohio; and in the Gallery of Flight Museum in Milwaukee.

When he isn't writing or modeling, Paul enjoys birdwatching, music, and travel.